GAN(‿

BIRMINGHAM

The Rise and Fall of the Burger Bar Boys

L. Brickley

This book is dedicated to the many young people and families who suffered through some of the most brutal times Birmingham has ever known. Some names in this book were changed to protect the identities of those involved; other names were changed out of respect.

CONTENTS

INTRODUCTION

Every city has its underbelly, a clandestine world operating in the shadows of civilization, unbeknownst to most who walk its streets. Birmingham, a city nestled in the heart of England, is no different. In "Gangland Birmingham: The Rise and Fall of the Burger Bar Boys," you are taken on an in-depth journey through the grim and chilling world of one of the most notorious gangs in the United Kingdom - the Burger Bar Boys. This exploration delves deep into the machinations of gang life, illustrating the brutal realities and repercussions that stem from the power struggles, criminal activities, and societal issues connected with the gang's reign.

The rise of the Burger Bar Boys was not an overnight phenomenon. It was a slow, grinding process born out of desperation, poverty, and a burning desire for power and respect. The initial chapters of the book are devoted to understanding this, as we peel back the layers of the gritty urban environment that bred and nurtured these hardened criminals. We navigate through the complex maze of Birmingham's streets, getting a sense of the significant geographical areas under the gang's control. Each territory, a strategic piece of the gang's dominion, echoes the gang's influence and reign of fear.

The initiation rites into the gang culture form a vital part of the narrative. The Burger Bar Boys was not just a gang but a brotherhood bonded by blood and violence. The initiation ceremonies were not just rituals but a rite of passage that marked the birth of new soldiers in this urban warfare. This brutality symbolised the harsh realities of the gang life and the lengths its members were willing to go to attain power and respect.

The Burger Bar Boys were notorious for their deadly use of firearms. Gunplay was not just a tool for them; it was an embodiment of their ferocious intent, a testament to their dominance, and an ever-present reminder of the power they wielded. The guns were a cornerstone of their operations, often playing a decisive role in their criminal activities.

One of the most gripping sections of the narrative is the exploration of the infamous Aston shootings. This tragedy served as a gruesome epitome of the gang's unbridled savagery. The aftermath sent shockwaves through the city, marking a significant turning point in the public's perception of the gang and triggering a vigorous response from law enforcement.

Drug trafficking, an operation that many gangs worldwide resort to, played a significant role in the Burger Bar Boys' story. The gang was deeply entrenched in this dark business, the profits of which served to bolster their power and influence. Understanding the mechanics of this trade and its impact on the community becomes a crucial part of comprehending the gang's hold over Birmingham.

Every gang has its own set of unwritten laws, and the Burger Bar Boys were no different. This exploration takes you into the code of silence or 'omertà,' an honour code that further strengthened the gang's unity and loyalty. This code of silence was not just an essential part of their ethos, but a survival strategy that protected the gang from the prying eyes of law enforcement and rival gangs.

Another fascinating aspect of the narrative is the examination of the gang's bitter rivalry with another notorious Birmingham gang - the Johnson Crew. This rivalry, which spanned years and claimed countless lives, became synonymous with the gang warfare that ravaged the city of Birmingham.

A particularly harrowing part of the story involves the gang's exploitation of children, their recruitment as 'child soldiers,' and their roles in the gang's operations. This disturbing insight highlights the extent to which the gang was willing to exploit the vulnerable for its operations.
The gang's impact on the community was as widespread as it was destructive. The activities of the Burger Bar Boys left an indelible mark on Birmingham, instilling fear, escalating crime rates, and

affecting public safety. Understanding this impact is key to assessing the scale of the devastation left in the wake of the gang's reign.

While male members dominated the Burger Bar Boys, the role of females within this gang was a complex one. Often unseen but not unimportant, the involvement of women in the gang presents another intriguing facet to the narrative, showcasing the insidious reach of the gang culture.

In the face of this gang's notorious reign, law enforcement eventually launched a significant crackdown, employing various strategies to counter the gang's activities. This aspect of the narrative presents an intriguing cat and mouse game between the police and the gang members, a relentless pursuit that eventually led to significant arrests and trials.

Perhaps the most hopeful part of this exploration is the stories of redemption, the tales of former gang members who managed to break free from this life of crime and rebuild their lives. These stories serve as beacons of hope amidst the chaos, highlighting the possibility of change and the power of resilience.

Gangland Birmingham doesn't shy away from discussing the Burger Bar Boys' influence on popular culture either. Their notorious reputation resonated within the music and film industry, creating a grim, yet fascinating portrayal of their lives and their impact on society.

Despite the eventual decline and fall of the Burger Bar Boys, their legacy is not easily forgotten. They left a city forever changed in their wake, their actions leading to lasting effects on Birmingham and its people. This final part of the journey reflects on these lasting effects and the ongoing efforts to heal the community and move forward.

"Gangland Birmingham: The Rise and Fall of the Burger Bar Boys" is a true crime exploration that takes you on a thrilling and sombre journey, illuminating the darker side of Birmingham's history. It invites readers to delve deep into the sinister world of gang life, all while uncovering the sobering realities that such existence brings.

This book is not just a tale of a notorious gang; it's a reflection of society, a commentary on our urban realities, and a testament to the human capacity for both violence and resilience.

GROUND ZERO: THE BIRTH OF THE BURGER BAR BOYS

Stepping into the pages of Birmingham's history in the late 1980s is akin to journeying into a labyrinth of contrasting extremes. A city with a proud heritage, located at the heart of England, it was a landscape of both breathtaking beauty and grim realities. Home to a bustling industrial sector and a vibrant cultural scene, Birmingham was a city pulsating with life. Yet beneath this lively façade, it harboured the breeding grounds of a gang that would soon send ripples of fear and violence through its streets - The Burger Bar Boys.

In the late '80s, the socio-economic landscape of Birmingham was riddled with challenges. The city was grappling with the aftermath of the industrial decline, a nationwide recession, and rising unemployment rates. Traditional jobs were disappearing rapidly, replaced by unsteady, low-wage work that left many families teetering on the edge of poverty.

The neighbourhoods of Handsworth, Aston, and Lozells bore the brunt of these circumstances. Populated predominantly by families of Afro-Caribbean descent, these areas were rife with racial tensions, economic disparities, and social exclusion. This cocktail of hardships created an environment of frustration and despair, particularly among the youth.

Life for young people growing up in these parts of the city was challenging. Opportunities for advancement were scarce, and prospects of a prosperous future seemed dim. Education was often disrupted by the need to contribute financially to the family or was seen as an unnecessary luxury when survival was the immediate concern. These conditions often resulted in young people dropping out of school, further reducing their chances of escaping the vicious cycle of poverty.

Youth centres and social programs that could have provided a safe haven and valuable resources were severely underfunded, leaving a void in these communities. With no place to turn to for support or guidance, many of these young people found themselves lost and vulnerable. It was in these vacant lots, rundown parks, and graffiti-covered back alleys that friendships were formed, alliances were built, and the foundation of what would become the Burger Bar Boys began to take shape.

Adding fuel to the fire was the dramatic increase in crime rates during this period. Birmingham was wrestling with a surge in violent crime, drug trafficking, and burglaries. The local police force, overwhelmed and understaffed, often struggled to contain this rising tide of lawlessness. The authorities were viewed with suspicion and resentment in these neighbourhoods, creating an even wider chasm between the police and the communities they were supposed to protect.

Drug addiction was another scourge that haunted these neighbourhoods. The emergence of crack cocaine in the late '80s had a devastating impact, turning once vibrant communities into zones of despair. This potent and highly addictive drug not only claimed numerous lives but also spawned a lucrative drug trade. As demand soared, drug trafficking became a profitable venture for those willing to take the risk. This illicit trade offered a glimmer of prosperity amidst a sea of deprivation, tempting many towards a life of crime.

In the midst of this grim reality, the gang culture began to take root. Gangs offered a sense of belonging, a promise of protection, and an avenue to quick money for the disenfranchised youth. As the allure of gang life began to take hold, petty crimes started to escalate into more severe offences. Violent assaults, armed robberies, and drug-related offences became increasingly common, marking the early signs of the chaos that was about to ensue.

This was Birmingham in the late '80s - a city steeped in economic struggle, social unrest, and rising crime. It was within these turbulent circumstances that the Burger Bar Boys found their genesis. The frustrations, struggles, and yearnings of the youth in these beleaguered neighbourhoods were about to find a violent outlet. Little did anyone realise then that the upheavals of the late '80s were just the prelude to a far more menacing saga that was about to unfold in the streets of Birmingham.

The term 'Burger Bar Boys' conjures up an image of a formidable gang that wreaked havoc on the streets of Birmingham. But before this notorious name became synonymous with fear and violence, it represented a group of individuals. They were young men who emerged from the tough neighbourhoods of Birmingham, each with their own stories, aspirations, and struggles that eventually led them to form the gang. These early players, whose actions would create a ripple effect of repercussions, were the gathering storm on the horizon of Birmingham's urban landscape.

One of the pivotal figures in the formation of the Burger Bar Boys was a young man known only by his street name, 'Zilla.' Born and raised in the economically disadvantaged neighbourhood of Handsworth, Zilla's story was one of hardship and adversity. Raised by a single mother who worked multiple jobs to make ends meet, he had experienced firsthand the relentless grip of poverty. A school dropout by the age of 15, his dreams of a better life seemed increasingly distant. Faced with an absence of viable opportunities and the allure of quick money, Zilla gravitated towards the drug trade, a choice that would set him on a path leading to the formation of the Burger Bar Boys.

Another key player in the formation of the gang was 'Dreads.' Dreads was a product of the Aston neighbourhood, another area notorious for its high crime rates and social problems. His father was absent from his life, and his mother was a drug addict, leaving him to navigate his way through a turbulent childhood largely on his own. His disillusionment with the system and resentment towards the lack of opportunities led him to a life of crime. His charisma, street-smarts, and fearlessness soon earned him respect in the local underworld, attributes that would later prove instrumental in his role within the Burger Bar Boys.

'Young Blood,' another future member of the Burger Bar Boys, hailed from the Lozells neighbourhood. Despite his tender age, he had already seen the darker side of life. His home was a battleground, with his parents engaged in a continuous struggle with drug addiction. Violence was a daily occurrence in his life, both at home and on the streets. Young Blood sought refuge in the camaraderie of his peers who shared similar experiences, their bond solidified by their shared struggles. The prospect of power and respect that gang life promised appealed to Young Blood, drawing him into the growing storm.

The fourth figure was 'Trigger,' a young man with a reputation for his hot temper and impulsive nature. Trigger was no stranger to violence. His aggressive tendencies, fueled by a challenging home environment, led him into frequent conflicts at school and eventually resulted in his expulsion. Disconnected from mainstream society and drawn to the sense of power that lawlessness offered, Trigger would become one of the most feared members of the Burger Bar Boys.

The formation of the Burger Bar Boys was not a single event but a process, a gradual coming together of these individuals drawn by shared experiences, aspirations, and grievances. Their paths began to cross in the late '80s, initially through casual interactions in their neighbourhoods and later in the darker alleys of Birmingham's underworld. Each one brought their unique personalities, skills, and motivations to the group. Zilla, with his leadership skills and strategic mind; Dreads, with his charisma and fearlessness; Young Blood, with his loyalty and desperation to escape his circumstances; and Trigger, with his raw aggression and reckless courage.

In their interactions, they found a shared sense of frustration towards a system they felt had failed them. They recognized a common yearning for respect, power, and financial security. They also discovered a mutual willingness to cross the boundaries of the law to achieve their goals. These shared elements acted as the glue, binding them together in a brotherhood that would eventually evolve into the feared gang known as the Burger Bar Boys.

In the backdrop of the turbulent social and economic landscape of Birmingham, these individuals found themselves at the eye of the gathering storm. Their frustrations, ambitions, and dreams, intertwined with the circumstances of their time, would serve as the sparks igniting the rise of the Burger Bar Boys. These early players stood at the precipice of a path that would lead to a notorious legacy. Their personal stories were set to become intertwined with the history of their city, leaving a mark that would echo through the streets of Birmingham for decades to come.

In the realm of Birmingham's underworld, the latter part of the '80s saw the emergence of a new force that would indelibly mark the city's history. This was the period that witnessed the genesis of the Burger Bar Boys, a collective formed out of shared struggles, ambitions, and a desire for power. Understanding the formation of this notorious gang requires delving into the mechanics of their early operations, the reasons behind their inception, and their initial impact on the community.

The origins of the Burger Bar Boys, as is often the case with many such collectives, were not borne out of a grand scheme but were rather the result of circumstances and personal histories coming together. Born out of the gritty realities of Birmingham's inner-city neighbourhoods, the gang offered an alternative identity to its founding members, a chance to assert their place in a world they felt had sidelined them.

The formation of the gang was a natural progression from the alliances that Zilla, Dreads, Young Blood, and Trigger had forged. This close-knit group, along with a handful of others sharing similar backgrounds and ambitions, began operating under a collective identity. The Burger Bar Boys' name was a somewhat mundane tag, derived from a popular fast-food joint where the group often met, discussed their plans, and shared their dreams. Yet, this seemingly innocuous name would soon become a symbol of fear and intimidation in Birmingham's streets.

The initial objectives of the Burger Bar Boys were as much about survival as they were about power. In a world where respect was hard to come by, they sought to command it through force and fear. They also aimed for financial prosperity, seeing the lucrative potential of the drug trade that was rapidly taking hold of their community.

Their early operations were an extension of the petty criminal activities they had previously engaged in individually, now coordinated and executed with a newfound sense of purpose and organisation. Drug trafficking quickly became their mainstay, with the gang members exploiting their knowledge of the local area and the burgeoning demand for narcotics. They also engaged in robberies and extortion, activities that not only bolstered their finances but also reinforced their growing reputation as a force to be reckoned with.

The recruitment strategy of the Burger Bar Boys during this initial phase was largely organic. New members were drawn from their network of friends and acquaintances, young men like themselves who were enticed by the allure of quick money and the sense of power that gang membership seemed to promise. They targeted the disaffected youth of their neighbourhoods, those who bore the brunt of societal neglect and yearned for a sense of belonging and purpose.

A key aspect of the Burger Bar Boys' early formation was the development of their code, an unwritten set of rules and expectations that guided their operations and internal dynamics. Loyalty was paramount, a principle that would later take on a lethal significance. Secrecy, a fierce commitment to their own, and an unyielding hostility towards rivals were other tenets of their code. These rules, enforced strictly and often brutally, helped consolidate their cohesion and control.

In these early days, the Burger Bar Boys' influence on the local community was a complex mix of fear and reluctant admiration. For many, the gang was a blight, a symbol of lawlessness and threat to public safety. Yet, for some, they were figures of rebellion against a system that had seemingly failed them. Despite the fear they incited, the Burger Bar Boys were seen by a few as a product of societal neglect, their rise a symptom of broader issues that had long plagued Birmingham's inner-city neighbourhoods.

Thus, the Burger Bar Boys came into existence, a manifestation of the frustrations, dreams, and desperation of a group of young men navigating a world they felt had turned its back on them. From their humble beginnings, they set out on a path that would lead them to infamous heights, their story an integral part of Birmingham's narrative. As we delve deeper into their journey, remember these formative moments – the sparks of their genesis – for they provide a vital understanding of the complex tapestry of circumstances, choices, and consequences that marked the rise of the Burger Bar Boys.

With this understanding, we can better navigate the tumultuous and often harrowing events that are to follow. We will explore the darker recesses of Birmingham's underworld, grappling with the forces of ambition, survival, and lawlessness that shaped the Burger Bar Boys' journey. In doing so, we'll uncover the startling realities of gang culture, revealing a world that is as fascinating as it is troubling, and as compelling as it is fraught with danger.

THE STREETS OF BIRMINGHAM: THE GANG'S TURF

To understand the rise and fall of the Burger Bar Boys, it is vital to understand the geography they controlled. The streets they ruled were not merely a backdrop to their story; these areas were both the stage and the fuel for their ascent. Their dominions, scattered across Birmingham, were pivotal in shaping their operations, their culture, and their influence. By mapping out their territory, we can comprehend the physical presence of the gang and the strategic importance of these locations.

The heart of the Burger Bar Boys' territory was located in the inner-city areas of Birmingham, particularly Handsworth, Lozells, and Aston. These neighbourhoods, with their tight-knit communities and intricate network of streets, became the nerve centre of the gang's operations. The Burger Bar Boys were products of these streets, and they instinctively understood the ebb and flow of life here. They exploited this knowledge, asserting control over these neighbourhoods and transforming them into their strongholds.

Handsworth, with its multicultural populace and economic disparity, was an area where the gang found a solid footing. They claimed these streets as their own, employing a blend of intimidation and streetwise charm to consolidate their power. They made their presence felt in Handsworth, transforming it into their bastion, a place from which they would plot their ascent.

Not far from Handsworth, Lozells and Aston provided the Burger Bar Boys with the room to expand their operations. Known for their vibrant communities and historical significance, these neighbourhoods were unfortunately also marked by high levels of unemployment, social deprivation, and crime. The gang seized upon these vulnerabilities, inserting themselves into the fabric of these areas, and their influence rapidly spread.

It wasn't just the residential neighbourhoods that fell within their sphere of influence. The gang extended their reach into commercial areas as well. The infamous Soho Road, a bustling shopping and business district, was under their purview. Here, the gang found a lucrative playground for their activities, especially their drug trade. This busy artery, with its constant flow of people, served as a discreet, yet profitable, marketplace for their narcotics operations.

Another significant location within their territory was the Perry Barr area, notably the sprawling grey complex of the Perry Barr Greyhound Stadium. This area held strategic importance for the Burger Bar Boys. Its network of backstreets and alleys provided the perfect cover for their activities. Furthermore, the hustle and bustle around the stadium, especially during race days, provided a convenient smokescreen for transactions that often went unnoticed by the unsuspecting crowds.

The Burger Bar Boys also exerted control over parts of West Bromwich and Smethwick, towns located on the outskirts of Birmingham. These areas were primarily used for storage and distribution of drugs, thereby keeping the main operational areas relatively clean and reducing the risk of police crackdowns.

The gang's dominions were not selected haphazardly. Each area held strategic significance, offering various advantages that the Burger Bar Boys exploited to strengthen their operations. The residential neighbourhoods gave them a community base, a ready pool of potential recruits, and a certain degree of legitimacy in the eyes of some locals. The commercial districts provided a venue for their illicit trade, while the areas on the outskirts acted as a buffer, helping them keep their core areas secure.

Their territorial claims were further reinforced by their use of graffiti, a typical method employed by gangs to mark their dominions. The Burger Bar Boys' tag - the three Bs - could be seen scrawled on walls, underpasses, and street corners, a clear and bold proclamation of their ownership.

The Burger Bar Boys' control over these areas was not merely about claiming physical space; it was a statement of power and defiance. They weren't just controlling streets and buildings; they were asserting their dominance over a society they felt had marginalised them. Their territory marked the landscape of their rebellion against the status quo, providing the foundations for their rise in Birmingham's underworld. As we journey further into their story, these geographical imprints will serve as key points of reference, spaces where the drama of their ascent and eventual downfall unfolded.

As the Burger Bar Boys established their dominions, life within these territories inevitably transformed. They brought about changes – some subtle, others glaringly apparent – that were both feared and begrudgingly respected by locals. Their influence over local life created a curious mix of terror, order, and a warped sense of community, reflecting the paradoxical nature of gang culture.

Within their strongholds, the Burger Bar Boys were a constant presence. They patrolled their territories, strutting down the streets with an audacious bravado that was both intimidating and captivating. Their distinctive attire, swaggering demeanour, and the three Bs insignia marked them out, announcing their presence and dominance. On street corners, in parks, outside local shops, their surveillance was continuous. They were always watching, asserting their authority at every turn.

This perpetual surveillance wasn't just about maintaining their control; it was also about the demonstration of power. The Burger Bar Boys often made public displays of their strength. Acts of violence became common, establishing their reputation as a force to be reckoned with. The streets under their rule bore witness to shootings, stabbings, and brutal beatings. Such brutal acts were both a show of force and a stark warning to those who dared to cross them.

Yet, amidst the violence, a warped form of order prevailed. The gang imposed its own set of rules within their territories. Drug deals, robberies, and other criminal activities were carried out with an uncanny level of organisation. The territories under their control became arenas of illicit economy, where lawlessness was the law. Even local businesses were not immune to their influence. Many were coerced into providing a cover for their operations, while others were taxed for 'protection.'

Life inside these strongholds was one of paradoxes. On one hand, there was fear and uncertainty; on the other, there was a strange form of stability, albeit one punctuated by crime and violence. To some in these communities, the Burger Bar Boys were a menace, their activities bringing turmoil and despair. Yet, to others, they were seen as providers of order, albeit through intimidation and brute force.

The gang's influence permeated all aspects of life in these areas. Schools were not immune to their reach. They would recruit young and impressionable students, enticing them with promises of money, respect, and a sense of belonging. These youths, often from disadvantaged backgrounds, were easy prey for the gang, and schools became breeding grounds for future gang members.

Their influence also extended to the local music scene. Birmingham's grime and rap culture were heavily affected by the gang's activities. Lyrics often referenced the Burger Bar Boys, their exploits serving as a form of street credibility. This infusion of gang culture into music further romanticised their image among impressionable youths.

The social fabric within these territories was under constant strain. Families lived in fear for their children, concerned about the allure of the gang life. Local authorities and social workers struggled to counter the gang's influence, their efforts often met with resistance from the gang and distrust from the community.

Yet, beneath the fear and instability, a sense of resilience emerged within these communities. Many locals resisted the gang's influence, standing up against their intimidation. There were instances of community members banding together, providing support to each other, and finding ways to safeguard their children. The local mosques, churches, and community centres often served as safe havens, offering solace and support amidst the turmoil.

Life within the Burger Bar Boys' territories was indeed a study in contrasts. These were places where fear and defiance, order and chaos, violence and resilience, coexisted. The gang's influence over local life was profound, reshaping the community's dynamics in ways that would have far-reaching implications. It's in this uneasy equilibrium that the next phase of the gang's story unfolds, a tale of rivalries, power struggles, and a city caught in the crossfire.

In the world of the Burger Bar Boys, territory equated to power. The streets they controlled served as the backdrop for their criminal activities, sources of revenue, and symbols of their influence. But as their dominions expanded, so too did their list of adversaries. These territories became battlegrounds for control, sparking off violent clashes that would eventually escalate into all-out gang wars. One conflict, in particular, would come to define their story – their bitter rivalry with the Johnson Crew.

The Johnson Crew, an established gang in Birmingham, had long held sway over several territories in the city. However, the emergence and aggressive expansion of the Burger Bar Boys threatened their stronghold. What began as minor skirmishes over territorial boundaries soon escalated into a full-blown feud, setting the stage for a bloody turf war that would grip the city's streets.

These conflicts were not merely about geographical boundaries; they were about power, respect, and the survival of the fittest in Birmingham's underworld. They often took the form of tit-for-tat violence, where an attack from one side would be met with swift retaliation from the other. Shootouts, drive-by attacks, and arson became common, turning some neighbourhoods into virtual war zones.

The Burger Bar Boys were unyielding in their defence of their territory and ruthless in their quest for expansion. They equipped themselves with an arsenal of firearms, turning to increasingly more violent methods to assert their dominance. Such was their resolve that they were often known to patrol their territories with a show of force, wielding their firearms with a chilling audacity.

The conflict also saw the introduction of novel and brutal tactics. 'Hotspots', as they were known, became a strategic tool. These were areas where the Burger Bar Boys would deliberately increase criminal activity to destabilise regions under the control of the Johnson Crew, intending to weaken their rivals and eventually take over.

At the height of the conflict, the gang's 'no-go zones' became a reality, with even law enforcement officers reluctant to venture into these areas. The Burger Bar Boys' stronghold, Aston, turned into one such zone, becoming a hotspot for gang-related violence and crime.

The turf war had a significant impact on the city. The crime rate soared as the two gangs fought for supremacy, leading to a climate of fear and uncertainty. Residents often found themselves caught in the crossfire, their neighbourhoods turned into battlegrounds. The unrest disrupted the local economy, reduced property values, and resulted in an overall decline in the quality of life.

Yet, amidst the chaos, the Burger Bar Boys continued to consolidate their power. They defended their territories, stood their ground, and with each successful defence, they seemed to grow bolder, further fueling their notorious reputation.

However, as the turf war waged on, it began to draw significant attention from the local authorities. The police, previously struggling to deal with the growing gang problem, started to focus their resources on the Burger Bar Boys and the Johnson Crew. This mounting pressure would lead to a significant turning point in Birmingham's gangland saga, setting the stage for law enforcement's response.

The territories of the Burger Bar Boys were thus more than just geographical locations. They were stages upon which power was contested, identities formed, and a city's history rewritten. The battles for Birmingham's streets were far from over, but the lines had been drawn, and the Burger Bar Boys had staked their claim.

The echoes of these territorial conflicts continue to reverberate through the city, their legacy imprinted in the communities that lived under the shadow of the Burger Bar Boys. As we delve deeper into the rise and fall of this notorious gang, we'll explore the dynamics of their power, the extent of their control, and the strategies they employed in their quest for dominance. This journey, though steeped in violence and fear, also offers insights into the complexities of gang culture, the societal structures that give rise to it, and the effects of gang activities on a community.

With every street corner that bore witness to their exploits, with every wall marked by their insignia, with every story told in hushed whispers, the saga of the Burger Bar Boys continues to unfold. The streets of Birmingham still echo with the tales of these turf wars, a testament to a time when the city was under the rule of gangland's notorious overlords.

BROTHERHOOD OR BLOODSHED: GANG INITIATION RITUALS

Birmingham, a vibrant city in the heart of England, has a unique blend of cultures, histories, and socio-economic realities. The late 1980s and 1990s brought a wave of transformations, some leading to prosperity and others leading to despair. Among the latter was the emergence of the Burger Bar Boys, a gang whose name would soon become synonymous with fear, power, and a peculiar sense of brotherhood.

Despite the danger and the notoriety, the allure of the Burger Bar Boys was powerful for many young men growing up in the deprived areas of Birmingham. Their reputation, the prospect of protection, and the lure of belonging to something greater than themselves were irresistible to some. This allure, though complex, can be traced to three principal elements: a desire for camaraderie, a need for security, and the appeal of power.

Camaraderie and a sense of belonging are inherent human desires. The reality for many young men in the economically struggling areas of Birmingham was one of isolation, whether due to broken families, inadequate education, or simple disillusionment with the prospects that society offered them. The Burger Bar Boys, for all their notoriety, offered a respite from this loneliness.

The gang provided a circle of friends, a surrogate family of sorts, who understood the realities of street life. These were individuals who, like them, had faced and were facing the harsh struggles that life in deprived areas posed. The gang was a brotherhood that shared their trials and tribulations, a group that was collectively against the world. This camaraderie and sense of belonging, regardless of the dangers it entailed, was intoxicating.

The second pillar of the gang's allure was the prospect of protection. Life on the streets of Birmingham was a hazardous affair, marked by violence, crime, and uncertainty. In such a climate, the promise of security held immense appeal. To wear the moniker of a Burger Bar Boy was to wield a shield of sorts, a deterrent to those who might wish harm. This security wasn't solely physical; it extended to a financial and social aspect as well. The gang offered a source of income, albeit from illicit activities, and social standing within their community. To some, this protection was a lifeline, a means of survival in a harsh world.

Power, the third cornerstone of the gang's appeal, is an intoxicating force. The Burger Bar Boys, at the height of their reign, held significant sway within their territories. They were figures of authority, arbiters of justice by their code, and to some extent, the rulers of their domains. This sense of power, of having control over one's destiny, was tantalising. It was a stark contrast to the feelings of helplessness and despair that often clouded the realities of their everyday lives.

Membership to the Burger Bar Boys was not merely about adopting a dangerous lifestyle; it was about being part of a unit, a fraternity. It was about the promise of a safer existence, a certain status within their community, and the allure of power. However, as the old adage goes, nothing comes for free. To gain these benefits, one had to pay a price, and the price was the initiation into the gang, a test of loyalty, courage, and ruthlessness, where failure was not an option, and success came at a high cost. But that is a story for another part of this chapter.

As we delve further into the world of the Burger Bar Boys, it's crucial to keep in mind the multifaceted nature of this phenomenon. The gang didn't exist in a vacuum. Their existence and appeal were the result of complex socio-economic and cultural factors that affected the city of Birmingham. This exploration is not an attempt to justify or glorify gang culture, but rather an effort to understand it better and highlight the conditions that make it possible. Because only by understanding can we hope to address the root causes and, in the process, maybe prevent the rise of such destructive forces in the future.

In the shadowy corners of Birmingham's deprived neighbourhoods, where the public's gaze seldom reached, a ritual took place that marked the crossing of a point of no return for many young men. The initiation rites of the Burger Bar Boys, cloaked in secrecy and fraught with danger, were a chilling rite of passage that ushered recruits into the notorious brotherhood. It was not a process to be taken lightly, as it demanded unflinching loyalty, courage, and at times, a complete disregard for one's own life.

Each gang has its initiation rituals, peculiar and varied. Yet, they all serve a similar purpose - to test the resolve, loyalty, and capability of the would-be gang member. For the Burger Bar Boys, initiation rites were designed to accomplish these ends, often pushing the initiates to the very brink of their physical and moral boundaries.

While the exact nature of the initiation rites varied, depending on the prevailing circumstances, the whims of the gang leaders, and the roles the new recruits were expected to fulfil, some elements were consistent. A common procedure involved an ordeal often known as "being jumped in." This violent ritual required the prospective member to withstand a timed, brutal beating from several existing members. The objective was twofold - firstly, to test the individual's physical resilience and courage, and secondly, to create a sense of 'indebtedness', owing one's membership to the collective and therefore strengthening the bonds of loyalty to the group.

Another ritual, far more chilling and morally repugnant, involved committing a crime, often a violent one. This could range from assaulting a rival gang member, participating in an armed robbery, or in extreme cases, carrying out a murder. The nature of the crime, often referred to as a 'mission', was typically assigned by a high-ranking member of the gang and was non-negotiable. These missions served several purposes. They acted as a proof of the individual's commitment and courage, created an aura of fear around the gang, and, most sinister of all, implicated the new recruit in a serious crime. This latter aspect was not incidental; it was a calculated move to bind the recruit to the gang. With a criminal record, the individual's prospects outside the gang would be severely limited, and the fear of retribution or legal consequences would further discourage any thoughts of leaving the gang.

Psychological manipulation was an essential aspect of these initiation rites. Often, the rites were orchestrated to ensure the prospective member felt both a profound sense of accomplishment and an overwhelming debt to the gang upon their completion. This delicate balance was crucial in ensuring the new members' loyalty and obedience.

Ceremonies and symbolism were also pivotal elements in the initiation rites. Tattoos featuring the gang's symbols, secret handshakes, and coded language all played a role in instilling a sense of unique identity and solidarity among the members. These symbols, often cryptic and complex, served as a constant reminder of the members' allegiance to the gang and further deepened the sense of separation from mainstream society.

While these rites might seem barbaric and senseless to outsiders, within the distorted reality of gang culture, they held profound significance. They were the gauntlet that separated the pretenders from the dedicated, the frail from the resilient, and the outsiders from the 'brothers'. This brutal selection process was a testament to the harsh realities of gang life, a life where power was paramount, and weakness, a liability.

These initiation rites, however harrowing and destructive, were but the opening chapter in the new recruit's life within the gang. Once initiated, the real test of their loyalty, tenacity, and ruthlessness would begin. Navigating the treacherous landscape of gang politics, rivalries, and the relentless scrutiny of law enforcement would demand far more than what the initiation rites could possibly extract. As we move further into the workings of the Burger Bar Boys, we shall explore these aspects of gang life in greater detail, revealing the grim reality beneath the allure of brotherhood.

In the aftermath of their gruelling initiation, the newly minted members of the Burger Bar Boys found themselves irrevocably bound to the gang. With each bruise earned, with each moral line crossed, they had been moulded into a piece of a formidable machine, a cog in a complex wheel of power, intimidation, and rebellion. The initiation rites, as harrowing as they were, served as their baptism of fire, a transformative process that seared the gang's code deep into their psyche.

The immediate impact of initiation on the recruits was multifaceted. Physically, they bore the brunt of their violent trials with their bodies often bruised, battered, and in some instances, permanently marked. Tattoos, a common part of the initiation ritual, became enduring reminders of their commitment, akin to military medals, they were worn with a perverse sense of pride and defiance.

On the psychological level, the effects were more profound and far-reaching. The initiation process was designed to desensitise the recruits to violence, making it a normalised aspect of their lives. The successful completion of the initiation rites often conferred a sense of achievement and belonging upon the recruits. They were no longer outsiders but 'brothers' in this closed society, lending them an elevated status among their peers and within their communities.

However, beneath this surface layer of newfound respect and camaraderie, there lurked darker consequences. Participation in violent crime and the fear of retribution, either from rival gangs or the law, forced them into a state of constant vigilance and paranoia. This state of perpetual anxiety, coupled with the guilt and trauma associated with their violent actions, often led to severe mental health issues. Depression, Post-Traumatic Stress Disorder, and substance abuse were commonplace among gang members, serving as a stark reminder of the toll gang life could take on an individual's mental well-being.

The culture and code of the gang were further reinforced by these initiation rites. Loyalty, courage, and an 'us versus them' mentality were paramount to the gang's survival. The initiation rites were a crucible where these values were tested and instilled. As these new members commenced their life in the gang, they found themselves woven into a complex hierarchy that demanded unswerving loyalty and absolute obedience. Any deviation from the gang's code was dealt with harshly, and punishments could range from public humiliation to more brutal forms of physical retaliation.

Moreover, the rites of initiation were not a mere introduction to the gang's code but also a stepping stone to the gang members' roles and responsibilities. Depending on their performance during the initiation and their perceived strengths, they would be assigned roles within the gang's operations. Some would become foot soldiers, tasked with defending the gang's turf and carrying out attacks on rivals. Others, with a penchant for strategy or a charisma that could influence and recruit, might climb the ranks to become leaders. This distribution of roles further reinforced the gang's structure and ensured the smooth operation of their illicit activities.

Ultimately, the initiation rites served as a chilling testament to the all-consuming nature of the gang life. The transition from initiation to active membership was rarely seamless. It was a journey fraught with danger, marked by violence, and shadowed by a constant threat to life. Yet, for those who survived, the initiation was also a source of pride, a symbol of their resilience, and a testament to their loyalty to the gang.

As we continue to explore the inner workings of the Burger Bar Boys, we lean further into this world where brotherhood is paid for in blood, and loyalty is measured in violence. We seek to understand, not justify, the reasons behind their actions and to shed light on a darker side of society that is often left hidden in the shadows. With each chapter, we aim to demystify the gang culture and, in doing so, hope to ignite discussions that can potentially lead to preventative measures and effective interventions. The tale of the Burger Bar Boys, as troubling as it is, serves as a stark reminder of the devastating impact of societal neglect and the desperate lengths individuals can go to when driven by a lack of opportunities and an abundance   of   despair.

GUNPLAY: THE GANG'S WEAPON OF CHOICE

In the gritty world of gangland Birmingham, power isn't just about controlling the streets; it's about controlling the narrative. It's about instilling fear, commanding respect, and fostering an image of invincibility. For the Burger Bar Boys, this image was, in no small part, shaped by the barrel of a gun. Firearms, in this context, were far more than mere tools of intimidation or enforcement. They became potent symbols of power and control, deeply embedded in the culture of the gang.

The significance of firearms in gang culture, particularly within the Burger Bar Boys, can be traced back to the socioeconomic conditions that prevailed in Birmingham during the gang's nascent stage. In the late '80s and early '90s, Birmingham, much like other industrial cities in the UK, was battling economic decline, high unemployment rates, and a growing sense of social disenfranchisement among its young population. It was within this cauldron of economic despair and social alienation that gangs like the Burger Bar Boys began to take root.

Firearms, at their most basic, offer a simple, albeit brutal, promise of power. In areas rife with crime and violence, where law enforcement was either absent or inadequate, possessing a gun meant possessing the means to not just survive, but to dominate. To the young men being drawn into the world of the Burger Bar Boys, a firearm offered a semblance of control over their otherwise chaotic and uncertain lives. It became a symbol of their defiance against a system that they felt had left them behind, a concrete representation of their willingness to seize power by any means necessary.

Within the gang, the importance of firearms was further magnified by their role in the power dynamics of the group. The ability to use a firearm, and more importantly, the willingness to do so, became a crucial factor in establishing one's standing within the gang hierarchy. It served as a metric of one's loyalty, ruthlessness, and commitment to the cause. This, in turn, played a pivotal role in creating a culture where violence was not just normalised, but glorified.

It's essential to understand that firearms, in the context of the Burger Bar Boys, were not merely tools of enforcement, but badges of honour. To carry a gun was to carry the weight of the gang's reputation, its collective power, and its unwavering resolve. It was a statement, a proclamation of belonging to a brotherhood that was bound by more than just shared circumstances; it was a brotherhood bound by a shared willingness to wield power, even if it came from the barrel of a gun.

The gang's fascination with firearms was also reflected in their operations. The Burger Bar Boys quickly gained notoriety for their brazen use of guns, both in their criminal endeavours and their battles against rival gangs. Drive-by shootings, armed robberies, and wanton displays of gunfire became trademarks of the gang, further solidifying their reputation as a formidable and ruthless entity.

It's important to remember that the gang's heavy reliance on firearms was also a response to their environment. In a world where violence was the language of the streets, guns were the words of choice. They were the means to enforce their will, to mark their territories, and to protect their interests. In the face of rival gangs similarly armed, firearms became an essential part of the gang's arsenal, a necessary tool in their fight for dominance.

Firearms, for the Burger Bar Boys, were thus much more than just weapons. They were symbols of power, respect, and control. They were an integral part of their identity and culture, a physical manifestation of their brutal approach to life and survival on the streets of Birmingham. This deep-seated association between the gang and their guns would not only define the Burger Bar Boys but also the city they operated in, casting a long, dark shadow of gun violence that would be felt for years to come.

In the underworld of the Burger Bar Boys, guns were more than mere instruments of power—they were a grim necessity, a means to an end in a world defined by survival of the fittest. The streets were an urban jungle, and the jungle demanded teeth. But how does a gang situated in the heart of Birmingham, where strict gun laws prevail, come to be armed and dangerous? This section sheds light on the shadowy processes by which the Burger Bar Boys acquired their firearms and the various criminal activities that were enabled and amplified by these weapons.

To understand the roots of the Burger Bar Boys' armed operations, we need to delve into the illicit firearm markets that fed the gang's arsenal. While the UK's stringent gun control laws made legal acquisition virtually impossible for the gang, the black market offered an alternate supply chain, enabling a steady flow of weapons into their hands. This clandestine market dealt in a wide variety of firearms, from handguns and semi-automatic rifles to more sophisticated high-calibre weapons. Here, a combination of international trafficking, local manufacturing, and reactivation of deactivated firearms played a crucial role in keeping the supply chain alive.

One of the primary sources of weapons was illicit international trafficking. Guns were often smuggled into the UK from Eastern European countries, where following the end of the Cold War, a surplus of firearms were available. These weapons were concealed ingeniously to evade customs, hidden within everyday items or disassembled and smuggled piece by piece, to be reassembled once they reached their final destination.

However, international smuggling was just one part of the equation. Closer to home, local criminal enterprises also contributed to the gun market. In some cases, 'antique' firearms, bought legally as 'curiosities or ornaments,' were modified to fire live ammunition. In others, deactivated firearms, purchased as 'safe' collectibles, were illegally reactivated, making them functional once again. These operations often required significant technical know-how, but they provided a steady stream of weaponry for gangs like the Burger Bar Boys.

The gang also used straw purchases—where a legal buyer purchased firearms on behalf of someone prohibited from owning them—to bypass restrictions. A member with no criminal record would buy weapons legally, only to hand them over to the gang. This method, though riskier due to the paper trail it left, was another way the Burger Bar Boys could amass their arsenal.

With a steady supply of firearms at their disposal, the Burger Bar Boys employed these weapons in a range of criminal activities. Guns were the cornerstone of their intimidation tactics, used to instil fear in rival gang members and civilians alike. Drive-by shootings, a notoriously brazen display of firepower, became a grim signature of the gang. These shootings not only served as a show of force but also as a means of marking territory, sending a clear message about who controlled the streets of Birmingham.

Guns also enabled the Burger Bar Boys to venture into more lucrative criminal activities. Armed robberies became a significant source of income for the gang, with banks, jewellery stores, and security vans often targeted. Firearms provided the gang members with the means to execute these high-risk, high-reward operations, bolstering their finances while further cementing their fearsome reputation.

In this grim dance of power and fear, guns were the dancers, leading the Burger Bar Boys deeper into the underworld. Every bullet fired, every weapon acquired, served to further entrench the gang in the criminal landscape of Birmingham, fueling a cycle of violence that was as devastating as it was enduring. The complex web of gun acquisition and the chilling efficiency of their use paints a stark picture of a gang determined to carve out its kingdom, no matter the cost.

The incessant echoes of gunfire on the streets of Birmingham were more than just an aural marker of the Burger Bar Boys' operations— they were the grim soundtrack of a city held hostage to violence. As the gang proliferated their use of firearms, the reverberations were felt far beyond the immediate victims. The impact, both direct and indirect, permeated through the fabric of the communities they operated in, shaping public perceptions, disrupting lives, and escalating the stakes in the gang's nefarious pursuits.

One of the most palpable impacts of the gang's rampant firearm usage was the surge in violence. The gang's decision to resort to firearms intensified confrontations with rival gangs, notably the Johnson Crew. What might have been contained as fistfights or minor skirmishes exploded into full-blown gun battles, turning the streets into war zones. Shootings became commonplace, with bystanders often caught in the crossfire. The death toll rose, each casualty a stark testament to the lethal turn gang rivalry had taken in Birmingham.

Simultaneously, the use of firearms magnified the gang's ability to instil fear. Guns served as psychological weapons, amplifying the gang's menace beyond their numbers. The knowledge that the Burger Bar Boys were willing and able to use firearms made them a force to be reckoned with, not just among rival gangs, but also within the communities they operated. The spectre of gun violence altered the very rhythm of daily life. People lived in fear, schools faced disruptions, and businesses struggled as footfall dropped. The psychological toll was as debilitating as the physical damage caused by the gang's activities.

However, the reverberations of the Burger Bar Boys' firearm usage were not confined to Birmingham's streets. The heightened violence and unrest caught the attention of the wider public, the media, and law enforcement. Newspaper headlines screamed about the 'Wild West Midlands,' and national news bulletins regularly featured updates on the 'gang war.' The Burger Bar Boys' reputation grew, far beyond their territorial boundaries, and so did the pressure on law enforcement to curb the escalating violence.

This public spotlight also brought the gang to the attention of policymakers. The rise in gun violence, particularly in Birmingham, led to an intensification of efforts to further restrict firearms and their illicit trade. New laws were considered and existing ones tightened, and resources were pumped into law enforcement and community initiatives aimed at disrupting the supply chain of firearms and providing alternatives for those at risk of falling into gang life.

However, all these responses seemed only to cement the Burger Bar Boys' reign of fear and power, as each headline and each news report only reinforced their chilling reputation. The guns in their hands were more than mere weapons—they were the instruments that enabled the gang to orchestrate a symphony of fear and control that echoed throughout Birmingham.

The Burger Bar Boys were no longer just another gang. Through their use of firearms, they had transformed into a formidable entity that symbolised the growing crisis of gang violence in the UK. In this saga of power, fear, and violence, the sound of gunfire was a recurring refrain, underlining the Burger Bar Boys' grim ascent into the annals of British crime history. It was a narrative that, much like the echoes of gunfire, would resonate long after the smoke had cleared, an indelible part of Birmingham's troubled legacy.

THE ASTON SHOOTINGS: A CITY IN SHOCK

In the early hours of January 2, 2003, the city of Birmingham hummed with its usual activity. Little did anyone know, the neighbourhood of Aston, otherwise known for its historic charm and industrial heritage, was about to be shaken to its core.

The evening started typically enough. The streets were busy with people returning home after work, local shops and food stalls were bustling, and the neighbourhood kids were playing football in the local park. Amongst them, two young girls, Letisha Shakespeare and Charlene Ellis, barely out of their teens, were celebrating New Year with friends. Known for their vivacious personalities, both girls were well-loved in the community, their futures seemingly full of promise and potential.

As the night wore on, the girls and their friends decided to attend a local party. The venue, a small salon on Birchfield Road, was teeming with young people, their laughter and chatter adding a joyful note to the otherwise chilly winter evening. It was a scene of innocence and normalcy, a snapshot of youth unburdened by the worries of the world. But in the shadows lurked an impending catastrophe that would cruelly shatter this scene.

Unbeknownst to the party-goers, members of the notorious Burger Bar Boys had been lurking in the area. Fuelled by an ongoing feud with rival gang, the Johnson Crew, the gang had been planning a retaliatory strike. Their target was not the innocent teenagers who were blissfully unaware of the danger, but rival gang members who they believed were attending the party. The weapon of choice was a firearm, an object that held a grim and significant presence in the gang's culture.

Just past 4 a.m., the cheerful chatter was pierced by the chilling sound of gunfire. In the blink of an eye, the party turned into a horrifying scene of panic and chaos. The deafening shots rang out through the night, a macabre symphony that echoed through the streets of Aston. Amidst the frenzy, four people lay wounded. Among them were Letisha and Charlene, who had been struck by stray bullets. The joyous celebration had turned into a nightmare.

The emergency services were on the scene within minutes, their flashing lights painting the street in harsh shades of red and blue. However, despite their best efforts, Letisha and Charlene succumbed to their injuries. Two promising lives were abruptly extinguished, victims of a senseless and violent feud that they had no part in. The grim reality of gang violence had taken its toll in the most tragic way possible.

The news of the shooting spread rapidly, the early morning silence broken by whispers of the horrifying incident. The Aston Shootings, as they would come to be known, had unfolded. The community of Aston was left reeling, struggling to comprehend the brutality of the incident. The tremors of the tragedy were just beginning to ripple through the city, setting off a series of events that would shake Birmingham to its core.

The dawn of January 2, 2003, brought with it a painful reality for the community of Aston. The neighbourhood, usually abuzz with life, was eerily silent. The usual morning routines were replaced with quiet whispers and shared glances of despair. The tragic events of the previous night hung heavy in the air, casting a pall over the city that was grappling with the senseless loss of two innocent lives. The streets of Birmingham had borne witness to violence before, but the brutality of the Aston Shootings had opened a wound that cut deep into the heart of the community.

In the homes of Letisha Shakespeare and Charlene Ellis, the morning brought an unbearable pain. Parents were forced to confront the unimaginable - the death of a child. Their agony, immeasurable and raw, echoed through the halls of their homes. The memories of their daughters were now etched in every corner, a stark reminder of lives that were full of promise but cut tragically short. Letisha's mother, a hardworking nurse, and Charlene's mother, a dedicated community worker, were thrust into the national spotlight, their personal grief exposed to the world.

The community rallied around the grieving families, their collective heartache spilling into the streets of Aston. Makeshift memorials sprung up around the city, adorned with flowers, pictures, and heartfelt messages for Letisha and Charlene. Residents young and old came together, united in their grief and their condemnation of the senseless violence that had claimed the lives of two of their own. Vigils were held, prayers were offered, and tears were shed, the collective sorrow a testament to the profound impact that the Aston Shootings had on the community.

The public outcry reverberated far beyond the streets of Birmingham. The nation watched in stunned silence as the horrific events unfolded in their living rooms, through the 24-hour news cycle. The Aston Shootings were not just another news story; they were a grim reminder of the terrifying reality of gang violence, a stark wake-up call that shook the nation to its core. The widespread coverage of the incident put the spotlight firmly on the Burger Bar Boys, revealing the terrifying extent of their criminal activities.

In the face of immense grief, a palpable fear hung over the community. Parents clutched their children a little tighter, the laughter of young ones was noticeably absent from the playgrounds, and a hush fell over the local schools. The streets, once a symbol of community and neighbourly bonds, were now shrouded in fear. Residents, both young and old, were forced to confront the reality of gang violence in their neighbourhood. A sense of vulnerability had settled in, the echoes of gunfire a chilling reminder of the danger lurking in their midst.

Calls for justice became increasingly loud as the days passed. The community, the city, and indeed the nation demanded answers. They demanded action. The grief-stricken faces of Letisha and Charlene's mothers became a poignant symbol of this demand for justice. The pain of their loss was echoed by the public, their cries for justice amplified by a community in mourning. The Burger Bar Boys, previously a name whispered in hushed tones, had been thrust into the spotlight, their violent deeds laid bare for all to see. The city of Birmingham, once known for its vibrant culture and industrial might, was now caught in the grip of fear and mourning. And as the cries for justice echoed through the streets, the stage was set for a city-wide confrontation with the terrifying reality of gang violence.

The brutal slaying of Letisha Shakespeare and Charlene Ellis on that fateful New Year's party in 2003 was more than a tragic incident; it was a catalyst that spurred a dramatic shift in public perception and triggered an unprecedented law enforcement response. The heinous crime was not just a moment of profound grief; it was also a moment of awakening, a defining event that would bring about an unparalleled focus on gang-related violence and the activities of the Burger Bar Boys.

In the days following the shootings, the city of Birmingham found itself at the centre of national and international media attention. Newspapers, television broadcasts, and online platforms were awash with headlines chronicling the grim events of the incident. The images of Letisha and Charlene, their youthful faces now emblematic of the horrors of gang violence, were beamed into homes across the country and beyond, the grim reality of their demise shocking the collective conscience of the nation.

The media storm played a pivotal role in igniting a public outcry against the escalating gang violence. In coffee shops, in workplaces, and on public platforms, people began to question how Birmingham, a city with a proud history and rich cultural heritage, had become a battleground for gangs. The outrage was palpable, leading to a public demand for an aggressive response to the gang menace that had been allowed to fester and grow unchecked.

The city's leadership was under tremendous pressure. The Aston Shootings were not merely another crime to solve; they represented a colossal failure of the system, a stark revelation of the city's inability to protect its youngest and most vulnerable. The city's law enforcement was called into question, prompting a swift and decisive response. The West Midlands Police, spurred by public outrage and media scrutiny, were forced into high gear. An extensive investigation was launched, with substantial resources devoted to bringing the perpetrators to justice.

As the probe into the shootings progressed, a chilling narrative began to emerge - one that unveiled the ruthless nature of the Burger Bar Boys and the horrifying extent of their criminal activities. The gang, previously a shadowy entity discussed in hushed whispers, was now exposed to the public in all its terrifying reality. The police raids, the court proceedings, and the relentless media coverage stripped the gang of its anonymity, bringing its actions under intense public scrutiny.

The judicial process, propelled by public sentiment and dogged investigation, was swift and uncompromising. The courts, often criticised for their leniency towards gang-related offences, seemed determined to make an example of this case. The unprecedented life sentences handed out to the four main perpetrators were hailed as a significant victory, not just for the bereaved families, but also for the city of Birmingham, marking a critical turning point in its struggle against gang violence.

In the aftermath of the Aston Shootings, the city of Birmingham underwent a transformation. The public outcry, the media spotlight, and the stringent legal response signalled a collective rejection of the rampant gang culture. The tragic incident had served as a wakeup call, leading to a concerted effort to eradicate gang violence and restore the sense of security in the city's streets.

The ripple effects of the Aston Shootings were profound. They marked a turning point in the city's battle against gang violence, triggering a series of events that would eventually lead to the downfall of the Burger Bar Boys. The chilling echoes of gunfire that rang out on that fateful New Year's Eve left an indelible mark on Birmingham, a painful memory that would forever remind the city of the grim reality of gang violence, and the crucial importance of ensuring such a tragedy never repeats itself. The story of the Burger Bar Boys was far from over, but the reaction to the Aston Shootings indicated that the tide was beginning to turn against the gang, setting the stage for the battles that lay ahead.

THE ART OF DRUG TRAFFICKING: THE GANG'S TRADE

As the decade of the 1990s dawned in Birmingham, it brought with it a wave of new opportunities for those operating on both sides of the law. On the fringes of society, in the overlooked corners of Birmingham, the Burger Bar Boys saw their golden ticket in the burgeoning drug trade.

Birmingham, with its expansive network of canals, diverse population, and strategic location, was a fertile ground for the spread of illegal substances. A dark underbelly began to emerge amidst the industrial heart of the United Kingdom. At the epicentre of this shift, ready to seize upon the growing demand for narcotics, were the Burger Bar Boys.

The gang's entry into the drug trade was not a haphazard venture but a calculated move, a strategic response to the socio-economic realities of the time. The late 1980s and early 90s were marked by high unemployment rates and social disarray, especially among the youth in Birmingham's deprived areas. Illegal drugs offered an escape for many, and the drug trade, in turn, offered an escape from the harsh realities of unemployment and economic deprivation for the gang.

Among the substances trafficked, two stood out: cannabis and crack cocaine. Cannabis, due to its widespread use and comparatively lower risks, became the staple commodity of the gang's drug enterprise. It was the foot in the door, the substance that allowed the Burger Bar Boys to establish a base of loyal customers.

However, it was the introduction of crack cocaine that marked a significant turning point. Crack cocaine, a powerful and highly addictive variant of cocaine, was a game-changer. With its high profit margins and intense demand, it quickly became the cash cow of the gang's illicit operations.

The rise of crack cocaine mirrored the increasing boldness and ambition of the Burger Bar Boys. Where cannabis allowed them to gain a foothold, crack cocaine accelerated their ascent, multiplying their profits and deepening their grip on Birmingham's criminal underworld.

The drug trade was not merely a source of income for the Burger Bar Boys; it was a means of expanding influence and consolidating power. The control over the supply of narcotics allowed them to wield substantial control over their territories. It led to a more profound intertwining of the gang's activities with the local community, as their influence seeped into every crevice of the areas they controlled. They had the power to determine who got a fix, who could deal, and who would remain on the outside, looking in. The drug trade had become their lifeblood, fueling their empire and entrenching their reign.

In this way, the Burger Bar Boys became a dual-edged sword within their community. On the one hand, they were the source of the very substances that offered a temporary escape from the harsh realities of life. On the other, their actions perpetuated a cycle of addiction and crime, further ensnaring those they claimed to protect.

The drug trade was far more than an economic venture for the Burger Bar Boys. It was a cornerstone of their identity, an essential part of their rise to prominence. It demonstrated their ability to exploit opportunities, adapt to their surroundings, and ruthlessly pursue their objectives. Their involvement in drug trafficking was an integral part of their story, a key chapter in their ascent from local nuisances to feared criminal organisation.

The drug trade of the Burger Bar Boys was an operation that required a level of organisation and sophistication that belied the gang's street-level origins. The mechanics of running a drug empire, from acquisition to distribution, demanded a structure that both ensured smooth operations and protected the key players from the prying eyes of law enforcement. The Burger Bar Boys, having embraced the brutal logic of the streets, demonstrated a keen understanding of these requirements.

At the core of their drug operations were the key players – the high-ranking gang members who acted as the linchpins of their narcotic network. These individuals, often shielded from direct exposure, had their hands firmly on the levers of the operation. They oversaw the procurement of drugs, managed the finances, and made strategic decisions about territories and distribution.

The acquisition of drugs was typically a complex process involving several layers of transactions to obscure the source. The Burger Bar Boys relied on an extensive network of connections that spanned across borders. The narcotics were usually purchased in large quantities to benefit from economies of scale, with payments made in cash to avoid leaving any traceable financial records.

Once the drugs were procured, the next step was the preparation for distribution. This was where the real 'art' of drug trafficking came into play. The raw substance, particularly in the case of crack cocaine, was often 'cooked' and converted into more consumable and marketable forms. This process was usually carried out in clandestine 'labs' or safe houses, set up in unsuspecting residential areas to avoid detection.

The distribution network of the Burger Bar Boys was both intricate and highly decentralised, designed to ensure that drugs reached the end consumers efficiently while minimising risks. The street-level dealers were at the bottom of this pyramid, selling the drugs directly to the users. These foot soldiers, often younger members of the gang or affiliates, bore the brunt of the risk, making them the most vulnerable link in the chain.

Territory was another crucial aspect of the drug trade. The Burger Bar Boys aggressively marked and defended their territories, ensuring a captive market for their drugs. They employed violence and intimidation to keep rival gangs at bay, leaving no stone unturned to maintain their monopoly over the drug trade in their areas.

Violence, in fact, was a tool frequently used in their operations. From ensuring compliance within their ranks to sending a strong message to rivals or potential informants, violence and the threat of it were integral to maintaining control over their empire. It was a language that the streets understood, and the Burger Bar Boys spoke it fluently.

Furthermore, they adopted several strategies to avoid detection and arrest. These included using minors who would face lighter sentences if caught, rotating drug stash locations, and employing lookouts to warn of law enforcement activities.

Despite their brutal and illegal modus operandi, the Burger Bar Boys built a system that thrived in the shadows. Their drug empire was more than just a criminal venture; it was a dark mirror to legitimate businesses, with its own hierarchy, logistics, and market strategies. The mechanics of their operation reveal a harsh yet fascinating insight into the depths to which the gang went to establish and maintain their dominance in Birmingham's underworld. It served as a testament to their adaptability, ruthlessness, and their unforgiving pursuit of power.

As with any activity, the Burger Bar Boys' engagement in the drug trade had a ripple effect on the broader community, leaving a trail of devastation in its wake. The echoes of addiction reached far beyond the boundaries of their territories, corroding the social fabric of Birmingham and engendering a climate of fear and despair. While the gang reaped the financial benefits of this illicit enterprise, the community bore the brunt of its destructive consequences.

One of the most profound impacts was on public health. The widespread availability of drugs like crack cocaine and heroin, both substances the gang dealt in, fueled addiction rates within the local community. These addictions, in turn, led to an increase in drug-related diseases, including HIV/AIDS and Hepatitis C due to shared needle use, and a surge in overdoses. Additionally, the mental health ramifications were severe, with a spike in substance-induced disorders and a resultant strain on local health services.

The impact on the community, however, extended beyond the realm of public health. The drug trade simultaneously exploited and exacerbated the socioeconomic challenges that many of the neighbourhoods in Birmingham faced. For some, dealing drugs for the Burger Bar Boys provided an alluring alternative to the limited economic opportunities available, despite the risk involved.

Young people, in particular, were drawn into this perilous web. The allure of quick money and the illusion of power and respect associated with the gang often proved irresistible to those feeling marginalised and disaffected. Yet, involvement with the gang often meant exposure to violence, criminal records, and, for some, a dramatically reduced life span. The gang's activities created a tragic cycle where the very conditions that made their drug trade profitable—poverty, disenfranchisement, and social instability—were further intensified.

The culture of violence that the drug trade nurtured also left indelible scars on the community. The gang-related violence, which often involved innocent bystanders, created an environment of fear and insecurity. Gunshots became a part of the night's soundtrack in some neighbourhoods, while tales of brutal retribution served as grim reminders of the perilous boundary that the gang had drawn around their operations.

The resulting fear affected every facet of community life. Parents were afraid to let their children play outside, while schools struggled with issues of truancy and disruptive behaviour linked to students' exposure to drug activity and violence. Local businesses, too, were impacted, with some closing down due to lost customers and others becoming unwilling participants in the drug trade.

Yet, amidst this tragic landscape, there were signs of resilience. Community leaders, faith groups, and local residents began to mobilise, organising rallies and campaigns against the drug trade and the violence it engendered. These efforts, though often fraught with danger, reflected the community's determination to reclaim their streets from the grip of the Burger Bar Boys.

Reflecting on the impact of the Burger Bar Boys' drug trade, it's evident that the echoes of their activities reverberated far beyond the corners they controlled. Yet, in these echoes are also heard the stories of those who resisted, fought back, and endured. Their stories serve as a reminder of the community's strength and resilience in the face of this adversity, a testament to the spirit of Birmingham amidst the storm. As the chapters of the Burger Bar Boys' reign close, these stories will be the ones that inspire the city's healing and reclamation, shaping Birmingham's narrative in the years to come.

THE CODE OF SILENCE: OMERTÀ IN THE STREETS OF BIRMINGHAM

Rooted in Sicilian traditions, Omertà is an unwritten code of conduct widely associated with the Italian Mafia. The ethos of Omertà dictates a strict adherence to silence about criminal activities, non-cooperation with authorities, and an unwavering loyalty to the 'family.' This pledge of silence has been romanticised and vilified in equal measure, etching itself firmly into the psyche of organised crime folklore. Yet, as we venture into the cold, rain-soaked streets of Birmingham, thousands of miles away from sun-drenched Sicily, the echoes of this clandestine promise can be heard resonating within the ranks of the Burger Bar Boys.

Founded in the late 1980s in Birmingham, the Burger Bar Boys emerged as one of the most formidable street gangs in the United Kingdom. Predominantly African-Caribbean, the gang had its unique dynamics and cultural nuances. Yet, intriguingly, it wasn't just the mafia's brutal reputation for violence and resilience that the Burger Bar Boys mirrored. In many ways, they had appropriated and adapted the concept of Omertà, weaving it into the very fabric of their operations.

Omertà, within the context of the Burger Bar Boys, manifested itself as an unwavering commitment to secrecy, loyalty, and solidarity among gang members. This encompassed everything from maintaining silence about the gang's activities to a refusal to cooperate with law enforcement. Furthermore, breaking this code, such as through acts of betrayal or talking to the police, was considered an affront to the gang and often met with severe reprisals.

For the Burger Bar Boys, Omertà went beyond being just a code of conduct. It was a binding social contract, an emblem of identity, and a mechanism to create and maintain order within the gang. This framework of silent allegiance was key to the gang's longevity and its ability to conduct its criminal activities with impunity. By embracing Omertà, the Burger Bar Boys created a protective shield, a buffer against external threats, particularly from law enforcement agencies.

In shaping their operations, Omertà served as a strategic tool that underpinned the gang's activities. From drug trafficking to armed robbery, the pledge of silence and loyalty ensured operational secrecy, minimised the risk of information leaks, and fortified their illicit empire. The code facilitated trust amongst members, which was crucial in a world where deceit could be deadly, and loyalty was more than a virtue – it was a necessity.

Omertà also played an instrumental role in shaping the gang's organisational structure and internal relations. The code of silence cultivated a sense of collective identity, reinforced the gang hierarchy, and bolstered the authority of the gang leaders. By adhering to the code, members demonstrated their allegiance to the gang, solidifying their place within the group while reinforcing the hierarchical order.

Yet, the adaptation of Omertà by the Burger Bar Boys was not a carbon copy of its Italian counterpart. Rather, it was a reshaping of the code to fit the unique socio-cultural dynamics of the gang and its surroundings. It evolved organically, shaped by the realities of gang life in Birmingham. While the core principles remained – silence, loyalty, non-cooperation with authorities – it was, in essence, Omertà reimagined through the lens of the Burger Bar Boys.

In the labyrinthine narrative of the Burger Bar Boys, the adaptation of Omertà offers a fascinating insight into the gang's operations and organisational structure. Yet, as we delve deeper into this unwritten code, we see that its implications stretch beyond the confines of the gang. The intricate dance between silence and loyalty, order and chaos, provides a unique window into the gang's influence on the broader community and the tumultuous world of Birmingham's streets.

While the pledge of silence encapsulates the essence of Omertà, it merely scratches the surface of the complex tapestry of the Burger Bar Boys' unwritten laws. These regulations, deeply embedded in the gang's culture, serve as both a guide and a set of boundaries for members. They navigate the intricate dynamics of respect, power, trust, and betrayal that underpin the gang's existence.

First and foremost, loyalty to the gang stands paramount. Any member of the Burger Bar Boys is expected to put the interests of the gang above all else. This includes their personal welfare, family commitments, and even their freedom. The gang, in many respects, is a family. However, unlike a traditional family, this bond is not based on blood relation but shared experiences, common goals, and mutual survival.

This loyalty manifests itself in various ways. For instance, when a member is arrested, the code dictates that they must not divulge any information about the gang or its operations, regardless of the personal cost. This 'no snitching' rule is one of the pillars of the Burger Bar Boys' version of Omertà. It is a binding rule that members are expected to uphold, with the threat of violent repercussions for those who dare to violate it.

Respect is another integral part of the gang's unwritten laws. Respect within the gang is a complex, hierarchical construct. New members must earn their respect through actions and loyalty, while those in the upper echelons command respect through power and fear. Disrespect, whether it be challenging a superior, failing to fulfil a task, or showing insubordination, is considered a grave offence. The punishment for such transgressions ranges from social ostracization within the gang to physical retribution, depending on the severity of the disrespect.

Conflict resolution is another area where the Burger Bar Boys' unwritten laws come into play. Inter-gang disputes, which are an inevitable part of gang life, are generally resolved internally, without recourse to external authorities. This may involve a mediated discussion between the conflicting parties, with senior members or the gang leader acting as arbiters. In some instances, though, violence may be used as a form of punishment or a way to restore balance.

Importantly, breaches of the code are treated with utmost severity. If a member is found to have violated the code, they are often subject to a 'trial' by the gang. This isn't a trial in the legal sense but rather an internal investigation led by the senior members. The gang member in question would have to explain their actions, and based on their defence, a punishment, often violent, would be meted out.

Another crucial aspect of the gang's code revolves around dealing with external threats. In the face of opposition or hostility, the gang stands united, presenting a solid front. This unity in the face of adversity further reinforces the gang's sense of brotherhood and collective identity.

To outsiders, these unwritten laws might seem brutal, extreme, or even inhumane. Yet, within the context of the Burger Bar Boys, they serve a critical function. These rules form the backbone of the gang's culture and provide a structured framework for their existence in a world that is otherwise characterised by chaos and uncertainty.

Understanding these laws, thus, provides a deeper insight into the mechanisms that drive the gang's operations and how they maintain order within their ranks. It also sheds light on the psychological dynamics within the gang and the social realities that such a lifestyle engenders. Yet, as we will see, the adherence to this code has far-reaching consequences, not just for the members, but also for the broader community that is entwined with the Burger Bar Boys' tumultuous journey.

The power of Omertà in the Burger Bar Boys' existence cannot be understated. It offered a sense of unity and order, a shared ethos that acted as a binding force for members, creating a protective shield around their illicit operations. Yet, like any social structure, it wasn't without its flaws and contradictions. The effects of this unwritten code of silence and honour were far-reaching, with repercussions not only within the gang but also rippling out into the wider community.

The strength of Omertà came from its effectiveness in maintaining the secrecy and security of the gang's activities. By enforcing a strict code of silence, the Burger Bar Boys ensured that crucial information regarding their operations remained within the confines of the gang. This hindered police investigations, making the gang's criminal undertakings harder to uncover and prosecute.

In this sense, Omertà acted as a facilitator for the Burger Bar Boys' criminal enterprises. The commitment to silence protected members from legal repercussions and allowed the gang to continue their illicit activities with relative impunity. This was especially the case with their involvement in drug trafficking and firearms, where the need for discretion was paramount.

However, despite these perceived benefits, Omertà was a double-edged sword. The same code that offered protection also brought about internal strains and conflict. The rigorous enforcement of the code often bred paranoia and mistrust within the gang. For instance, suspicions of snitching often led to internal investigations and punishments, resulting in an atmosphere of anxiety and fear.

Moreover, the strict adherence to Omertà sometimes created conflict between the gang's interests and personal ties. Members found themselves trapped between their loyalty to the gang and their relationships outside of it. This was particularly true when family members or close friends were impacted by the gang's activities. The emotional and psychological toll of these conflicts often led to dissent and even defection from the gang.

Perhaps the most significant strains emerged when the code was broken. Instances of betrayal, though rare, had dire consequences. They often led to a cascade of events including violent reprisals, power struggles, and increased scrutiny from law enforcement. For the individuals involved, the price of breaking Omertà was often paid in blood and profound personal loss.

Within the wider community, the effects of Omertà were decidedly negative. By fostering a culture of fear and silence, the Burger Bar Boys were able to operate relatively undisturbed. Their criminal activities continued to wreak havoc on the community, causing social unrest, exacerbating drug addiction, and escalating violence.

The Burger Bar Boys' adaptation of Omertà played a central role in shaping their operations, internal dynamics, and their relationship with the broader community. It formed the crux of their power, facilitating their criminal enterprises while also imposing a strict regime of silence and loyalty. Yet, it also presented significant strains, leading to internal conflict and contributing to the gang's eventual downfall.

As we learn more about the inner workings and external impacts of the Burger Bar Boys, it becomes clear that understanding their unwritten laws and the code of Omertà is key to comprehending the complex dynamics of this notorious gang. It is through these insights that we can begin to grasp the gravity of their impact on Birmingham and the intricate web of crime, loyalty, and power that defined their reign.

ENEMY LINES: THE BURGER BAR BOYS VS. THE JOHNSON CREW

The genesis of the rivalry between the Burger Bar Boys and the Johnson Crew has a deeply ingrained history, embedded in the sociopolitical landscape of Birmingham. The beginnings were relatively innocuous, both gangs springing up from common roots in the impoverished neighbourhoods of the city. Their common goal was survival, grappling with socioeconomic challenges, racism, and a lack of opportunities that ran rampant in these underserved areas. This shared struggle became the breeding ground for an alliance that would eventually fracture into a deadly feud.

The Burger Bar Boys and the Johnson Crew originally emerged as a collective response to their harsh surroundings. In the early days, they banded together, a unified front against common foes: poverty, discrimination, and rival gangs from other cities. Their affiliation was a symbiotic relationship, each member providing mutual protection and support, whilst indulging in petty criminal activities.

However, as the groups began to grow in size and ambition, internal fractures started to emerge. The shared ethos of camaraderie and mutual survival began to erode, replaced by greed, power struggles, and territorial disputes. With the introduction of the lucrative drug trade in the late 1980s, what was once a brotherhood morphed into competing business interests.

The Burger Bar Boys and the Johnson Crew began operating in distinct territories. The Burger Bar Boys claimed the neighbourhoods of Handsworth, Soho Road, and Lozells as their own, while the Johnson Crew held sway over Aston and Perry Barr. These areas were riddled with low-income housing, high unemployment rates, and a prevalent drug problem, which offered a ready market for their illicit activities. Territory was everything – it equated to customers, power, and respect.

The split was not a clean break. There were altercations, skirmishes over contested areas, and disagreements over their operations. Each confrontation further deepened the divide, slowly cementing their status as rivals rather than allies. A major point of contention was the drug trade, where competition over customers turned violent.

The escalation from discord to a deadly gang war was a gradual yet relentless process. It was fueled by a series of tit-for-tat incidents, retaliatory attacks that became increasingly brutal and public. The animosity was no longer just about business or territory; it was personal. A profound hatred had been cultivated, permeating every interaction between the two gangs. The rivalry was now entrenched, the battle lines drawn in the heart of Birmingham. It wasn't just a fight for survival or supremacy; it was a vendetta written in the blood of their members.

While the exact catalyst for the outright warfare is hard to pinpoint, by the mid-1990s, the Burger Bar Boys and the Johnson Crew were sworn enemies. Street fights, drive-by shootings, and drug-fueled violence became a common occurrence in their respective territories. The hatred had seeped so deep that even the mere mention of the rival gang was seen as an affront, a direct challenge to their authority. The gangs were now on a collision course, the streets of Birmingham their battlefield, and the community held in the crossfire of their deadly feud. The genesis of rivalry had given way to an all-out war, the repercussions of which would be felt across the city and beyond.

The rivalry between the Burger Bar Boys and the Johnson Crew wasn't simply a dispute among individuals; it was a territorial battle, a violent struggle for dominance and control over Birmingham's streets. Their warfare was marked by relentless turf wars, strategic manoeuvres, and violent confrontations. Their conflict, embedded in the urban fabric, turned neighbourhoods into battlefields and the community into unwilling spectators of their feud.

The territories each gang controlled were more than just geographical markers; they represented influence, power, and wealth. For the Burger Bar Boys, their stronghold comprised the neighbourhoods of Handsworth, Soho Road, and Lozells, areas steeped in socioeconomic deprivation and rife with drug addiction, a ready market for their illicit trade. On the other hand, the Johnson Crew ruled over Aston and Perry Barr, neighbourhoods bearing a similar socio-economic imprint.

Territorial boundaries were clearly demarcated yet fluid, each gang constantly probing for weaknesses, looking for opportunities to encroach upon the other's territory. The frontline of their turf wars shifted through the streets and back-alleys of Birmingham, fluctuating with every minor victory or loss.

Violent confrontations were the hallmark of these turf wars. Gang members patrolled their territories, their firearms at the ready, their senses attuned to the faintest hint of a rival's presence. Drive-by shootings, armed ambushes, and brutal beatdowns became a grimly familiar part of life in these neighbourhoods. The currency of these battles was not merely territory, but also fear and respect. By demonstrating a willingness to commit violence, each gang sought to project power and deter the other.

Each side employed a range of strategies to undermine the other. In the deadly game of dominance, controlling the local drug trade was a critical objective. They employed tactics that ranged from violent intimidation of rival drug dealers to price undercutting to win over customers. The drug trade was not only a source of revenue, but also a weapon wielded to destabilise and weaken the opposition.

Another aspect of their strategy involved recruitment and grooming of young members. New recruits were enlisted from local schools and neighbourhoods, drawn in by the allure of easy money, status, and a sense of belonging. These new recruits were often used as foot soldiers in their turf wars, their youthful exuberance and desperation exploited in the service of the gang's objectives.

In the volatile dynamics of the turf wars, alliances also played a key role. Both the Burger Bar Boys and the Johnson Crew sought allies among smaller local gangs. These alliances, often fleeting and driven by convenience, were another tool in their arsenal, bolstering their numbers and extending their influence.

One cannot discuss the turf wars without addressing the grim toll it took on the community. Innocent residents lived in constant fear, their neighbourhoods transformed into war zones. The sounds of gunshots became a chillingly regular part of their reality. The turf wars led to a drastic increase in violent crimes, creating an atmosphere of tension and fear that held the community hostage.

The turf wars between the Burger Bar Boys and the Johnson Crew was not just a conflict; it was a systematic battle for dominance that exploited and scarred the very community it emerged from. Each clash, each shot fired, each life lost, marked another episode in their ongoing struggle, a deadly dance that held Birmingham in its cruel grip.

The gang warfare that unfolded between the Burger Bar Boys and the Johnson Crew had far-reaching implications, casting a long and intimidating shadow over the city of Birmingham. The impact was profound, with the tremors of their conflict resonating through the public safety, law enforcement, and social fabric of the city.

Public safety became a major casualty in the wake of their turf wars. The streets of Birmingham, especially the neighbourhoods controlled by the rival gangs, became sites of fear and uncertainty. Gunshots echoed through the night, people were afraid to venture out after dark, and parents worried about their children being lured into the gangs. The peace and tranquillity that should have characterised community life was shattered, replaced by the chilling spectre of violence and crime. The fear was palpable, the anxiety ever-present.

The escalation in gang violence placed an immense burden on law enforcement. The West Midlands Police found themselves grappling with a complex, multifaceted crisis. The increase in violent crimes strained their resources and posed a significant challenge to their crime-solving capabilities. Their task was further complicated by the gang's code of silence, which made gathering reliable intelligence and securing witness testimonies exceedingly difficult.

In response to the gang violence, law enforcement had to adapt their strategies. There was an increase in stop-and-search operations, surveillance was heightened, and more resources were allocated towards undercover operations. In 2003, Operation Ventara was launched, a targeted initiative aimed at dismantling the gang network. This operation led to numerous arrests, drug seizures, and weapons confiscations. While these efforts made a significant impact, they were often akin to fighting fires rather than addressing the root causes.

The gang warfare didn't just exacerbate crime rates; it amplified social issues within the city as well. Birmingham's communities, already grappling with challenges like unemployment, socio-economic deprivation, and substance abuse, found these problems amplified in the face of the gang violence. The constant state of fear and unrest impeded community development efforts and deterred investments, trapping many in a cycle of poverty and crime.

The gang warfare also had a profound psychological impact, especially on the city's youth. With their community dominated by the gangs, the young people found their perceptions and expectations warped by the violence and crime that was a part of their everyday reality. Many saw joining a gang as a means of survival, a twisted sort of aspiration nurtured in the crucible of gang warfare.

As the Burger Bar Boys and the Johnson Crew clashed, the collateral damage of their warfare was the city of Birmingham itself. The very streets where children should have been safe to play became battlegrounds, the communities turned into pawns in their game of power. The echo of each gunshot, the silence that followed each act of violence, was a stark reminder of the heavy price the city paid for their feud.

In retrospect, the warfare between the Burger Bar Boys and the Johnson Crew was more than just a conflict between two gangs; it was a blight on the city of Birmingham, a dark period in its history that left indelible scars on its communities. Yet, as history would reveal, even in the face of such dire circumstances, the spirit of Birmingham remained resilient. This challenging period forced the city to confront the systemic issues that gave rise to such violence, sparking a quest for solutions that went beyond law enforcement and delved into the heart of their communities. And in this resilience lies the true strength of Birmingham, a city that despite its wounds, never ceased striving for a brighter, safer future.

YOUNG KILLERS: CHILD SOLDIERS OF THE BURGER BAR BOYS

The darkness of gang culture often thrives in the shadowy corners of society, but when it begins to reach into the realm of childhood and rob young ones of their innocence, it is a disturbing violation that cuts deep. The Burger Bar Boys, not unlike many street gangs worldwide, found in the recruitment of children a strategic advantage that would serve multiple purposes. Their approach was both ruthless and cunning, a testament to their willingness to exploit vulnerability for the advancement of their criminal activities.

To understand the forces that drive children into the arms of a street gang like the Burger Bar Boys, we must first turn our gaze toward the socio-economic circumstances prevailing in the areas of Birmingham where the gang primarily operated. Economic deprivation, coupled with high rates of unemployment, created conditions ripe for the breeding of discontent, disenfranchisement, and despair. These neighbourhoods were often characterised by poverty, poor housing, low educational attainment, and a lack of opportunity - a cocktail of factors that can lead the youth astray.

For many children growing up in these conditions, the allure of gang life can be intoxicating. The prospect of power, respect, and wealth, no matter how ill-gotten, stands in stark contrast to the bleak futures they foresee for themselves. The gang promises a sense of belonging, a chance to rise above their circumstances, and an opportunity to wield the power they so often see used against them.

The family backgrounds of these children often play a crucial role in their susceptibility to gang recruitment. Those from broken homes, where parental supervision is lacking, or where family members themselves are involved in criminal activities, are particularly vulnerable. The gang, in many ways, steps in to fill the void, offering a perverse sense of family and community. It's a toxic surrogate for the nurturing environment these children lack, but for them, it's a lifeline in an ocean of uncertainty.

The community influences are just as potent in steering these young lives towards gang culture. When children grow up seeing gang members as the most successful figures in their community, it skews their perception of success and normalises a life of crime. In the absence of positive role models, the young minds idolise the gang members, who parade their ill-gotten wealth and command respect through fear.

Recruitment is often subtle, a gradual process that starts with simple tasks to prove their worth, like acting as lookouts or running errands. The child is slowly introduced to the gang's activities, becoming desensitised to the violence and criminality, a slow but sure descent into the gang's clutches. As they prove their loyalty and usefulness, they are assigned more significant tasks, from drug trafficking to weapon carrying, and in some cases, even violence.

The recruitment of children by the Burger Bar Boys showcases the predatory nature of the gang. It also underscores the desperate need for social interventions aimed at breaking the cycle of crime and poverty, and creating safer, more nurturing environments for children. However, these interventions alone would not be sufficient. They would need to be paired with efforts to dismantle the structures of the gang, a task that law enforcement would grapple with, in their pursuit to restore peace and order to the streets of Birmingham.

When children are entangled in the nefarious web of the Burger Bar Boys, they become embroiled in a life that is as dangerous as it is damaging. The roles they are entrusted within the gang speak volumes about the chilling nature of this exploitation, which is strategic, systematic, and profoundly harmful.

Upon entering the gang, children are often assigned roles based on their age, physical prowess, and, perhaps most importantly, their capacity to elude law enforcement scrutiny. Their relative invisibility to the police and their malleability make them desirable pawns in the gang's criminal operations.

A significant number of these children are drawn into drug trafficking. Their size and age, which would typically signify vulnerability, are strategically used to the gang's advantage. They're often dispatched as couriers, transporting drugs between different parts of the city. Their harmless appearance provides an effective camouflage, enabling them to slip under the radar of law enforcement. They might also be employed as street-level dealers, peddling drugs under the watchful eyes of their older gang members.

The manipulation doesn't end at merely using the children for the gang's operations; there is also a significant level of conditioning involved. The children are exposed to a reality warped by the gang's norms, where criminality is not only normalised but glorified. Coercion and indoctrination play a significant role in ensuring these young recruits remain loyal to the gang. Rewards, punishments, and peer pressure are manipulated with chilling precision, ensuring that the children are both fearful and in awe of their older counterparts.

Regrettably, the roles assigned to these children are not confined to drug trafficking. As they are further steeped in gang culture, some of them become involved in more violent aspects of gang activity. Acting as lookouts during violent confrontations, or even being pushed to participate directly in violent acts, are not uncommon occurrences. Instances where children are used as human shields or are ordered to carry out hits underline the horrifying extent of the gang's exploitation.

A particularly troubling aspect of this exploitation is the way the Burger Bar Boys and other similar gangs use these children to evade law enforcement. By placing them on the front lines of their illegal operations, the gang leaders insulate themselves from immediate risk. The children, with their futures stolen and innocence shattered, bear the brunt of law enforcement action while the puppet masters stay shrouded in the shadows.

The gang, in its pursuit of power and wealth, moulds these children into replicas of themselves. The brutal reality is that the Burger Bar Boys created a production line of young criminals, destined to follow in their footsteps if left unchecked. This chilling reality underscores the importance of timely intervention, offering these children an alternative to the path of crime, and providing opportunities that allow them to extricate themselves from the grip of the gang.

The world of the Burger Bar Boys is a sinister one, marked by violence, crime, and a blatant disregard for the law. But for the children ensnared in this life, the consequences extend far beyond the immediate dangers that they face on the streets. The impact of their involvement with the gang reverberates across all aspects of their lives, casting long, menacing shadows on their future.

The psychological trauma experienced by these children is profound. The violence they witness and sometimes participate in leaves an indelible mark on their mental health. Anxiety, depression, and post-traumatic stress disorder (PTSD) are not uncommon among these young recruits. The world they inhabit is one of paranoia and fear, where each day brings a new set of dangers. The relentless pressure to conform, the threat of violent retribution if they falter, and the constant dread of law enforcement or rival gangs result in a state of chronic stress that hampers their mental and emotional development.

Physically too, these children face significant risks. Exposure to substance abuse, violence, and sexual exploitation result in a host of health issues. The dangerous tasks they are charged with, such as drug trafficking or involvement in violent skirmishes, place them in situations of direct harm. They live their lives in a state of perennial risk, their young bodies bearing the brunt of the gang's ruthless activities.

The toll on their education and overall development is equally severe. School often takes a back seat to gang duties, resulting in low academic achievement, school dropouts, and limited prospects for higher education or stable employment. This creates a vicious cycle, trapping them further in the life of crime as their options to break away diminish.

However, the implications of this child exploitation extend beyond the individual children; it is a societal problem with far-reaching ramifications. These child soldiers of the Burger Bar Boys pose significant challenges for social services, law enforcement, and educational institutions.

Social services are faced with the enormous task of rehabilitating these young victims of gang exploitation. Providing them with the necessary mental health support, helping them reintegrate into society, and equipping them with the skills to lead a life away from crime requires resources, expertise, and a long-term commitment.

For law enforcement, these children represent a complex dilemma. On one hand, they are perpetrators of crime, on the other, they are victims of exploitation. Striking a balance between punitive action and protective measures becomes a delicate task. Law enforcement agencies have to devise strategies that disrupt gang activities without causing further harm to these young victims.

Educational institutions are also deeply affected. Schools may become hotspots for recruitment or gang-related activities, disrupting the educational environment. Teachers and administrators have to grapple with maintaining safety and ensuring that these children don't fall through the cracks of the educational system.

As this chapter draws to a close, it's important to remember that the child soldiers of the Burger Bar Boys represent a failure of society as a whole. The narrative of these children is a stark reminder of how imperative it is to invest in our communities, support our children, and provide the necessary safeguards to prevent such exploitation. The rise and fall of the Burger Bar Boys serve as a chilling testament to the lengths human beings can go when left with limited choices and resources.

Understanding their story is not about justifying their actions or romanticising their life of crime. It's about learning from their trajectory, about recognizing the signs when a child is veering off course, about stepping in before it's too late. Because every child saved from the clutches of a gang is a step towards a safer, kinder, and   more   equitable   society.

BITTER LEGACY: THE IMPACT ON BIRMINGHAM'S COMMUNITY

Living under the constant shadow of the Burger Bar Boys had profound psychological implications on the residents of Birmingham, particularly those dwelling in the direct sphere of the gang's influence. The seemingly omnipresent threat of violence and crime dictated the ebb and flow of daily life, casting a chilling pallor over the community's collective psyche. The anecdotal accounts and testimonials of those who lived through this era serve as stark reminders of the human toll inflicted by the gang's reign.

Take for instance, the account of Alice, a long-time resident of Handsworth, an area with a strong gang presence. "I've lived in Handsworth for over 30 years," she shared, "but it was during the height of the Burger Bar Boys' reign that I truly felt afraid to live in my own home." The safety of the community, once taken for granted, had been replaced with an overwhelming sense of dread that would grip the residents of Handsworth as the sun set, ushering in the uncertainty of night.

The fear was not restricted to the gang's prime hours of operation. Even in daylight, anxiety shaped the community's behaviour. Parents were fearful of letting their children out to play. Local shop owners faced the constant threat of theft and damage. Simple activities like going to the local shops, catching a bus, or even standing in one's garden became fraught with fear.

Schools in the gang's territories were particularly affected, as they became hotspots for recruitment and intimidation. Teachers reported students exhibiting signs of stress, anxiety, and depression, with school performance suffering as a result. Many of these children were exposed to violence, either directly or indirectly, with profound implications for their mental health.

Sarah, a school teacher in one such school, recalled, "Many of the children were scared. They saw things that no child should ever witness. This had a massive impact on their school life. Many couldn't concentrate in class; they were anxious, constantly looking over their shoulders."

The profound impact on mental health extended beyond direct victims of the gang's activities. Even those not directly targeted by the gang were subjected to the fear that permeated the community. As one resident said, "Even if you weren't directly involved, you knew what was happening. You heard the stories, saw the police, heard the sirens. You always wondered if you were going to be next."

As a mental health professional working in Birmingham during this period noted, "This constant state of high alert is incredibly damaging. It's akin to living in a war zone. The ongoing stress and fear take a toll, leading to a range of mental health issues, including PTSD, anxiety disorders, and depression."

The accounts, testimonials, and professional insights paint a vivid picture of the impact of living under the Burger Bar Boys' reign of fear. The stories speak not just of physical violence, but of a community held hostage by fear, of children growing up too quickly, and of a society living on the edge, forever anticipating the next outbreak of violence. The emotional trauma of this period left lasting scars on the psyche of the Birmingham community, a reminder of the darkness that once enveloped their lives under the shadow of the Burger Bar Boys.

The ascendency of the Burger Bar Boys in Birmingham wasn't a silent phenomenon; it was marked, tellingly, by an increase in crime rates throughout the city. The shadow of violence that the gang cast over the community was more than just psychological; it left tangible, devastating traces in its wake. Crimes, from minor offences to heinous acts of violence, grew exponentially during the peak years of the gang's reign, leaving residents in a state of perpetual fear and the city's law enforcement overwhelmed.

As the gang's influence in the city began to consolidate, a corresponding surge in crime followed. According to crime data from West Midlands Police, areas with a strong gang presence, including Aston, Handsworth, and Lozells, experienced a significant uptick in violent crime during the height of the gang war. Gun crime, in particular, soared. The grim moniker "Gunchester," coined by the press in reference to Manchester's own struggle with gun crime, began to feel uncomfortably apt for Birmingham as well.

Drug-related crimes also saw a sharp rise. Drug trafficking, possession, and crimes related to drug misuse became increasingly common as the Burger Bar Boys expanded their narcotics empire. As one former officer put it, "It was like trying to stem a tidal wave with a tea strainer. We were perpetually playing catch-up."

The repercussions were not limited to direct criminal activities. The gang's operations spawned a range of associated crimes. To fund their drug habits, addicts committed thefts, burglaries, and muggings, escalating the fear and insecurity that plagued Birmingham's communities. Similarly, as the gang sought to exert their dominance, vandalism, and arson attacks spiked, leaving residents in constant fear for their property and lives.

The repercussions on public safety were immediate and severe. Previously bustling streets became deserted after dark, local businesses suffered as people were reluctant to venture out, and community events dwindled as fear of potential violence kept people at home. Parks and public spaces, once the heart of the community, were abandoned, viewed as potential hotspots for gang activities.

This wave of crime and the resulting fear posed significant challenges for law enforcement. Police resources were stretched to breaking point. Officers found themselves constantly in reactive mode, racing from one crime scene to another, with little time or resource for proactive community policing or prevention work. Moreover, the willingness of the Burger Bar Boys to use serious violence, including firearms, put immense strain on police officers, many of whom found themselves dealing with levels of crime and violence they had not been trained to handle.

But beyond the operational challenges, perhaps the most significant impact on law enforcement was the erosion of public trust. Many residents felt that the police were unable to protect them, a sentiment that was compounded by the omnipresence of the Burger Bar Boys. This feeling of abandonment led to further divisions between the community and the police, a divide the Burger Bar Boys were all too willing to exploit.

Through this examination of crime rates and their impact on public safety, the wide-reaching and lasting impact of the Burger Bar Boys becomes clear. Their reign was not merely an isolated period of heightened gang activity; it was a crisis that permeated every aspect of Birmingham's communities, leaving behind a legacy of fear, mistrust, and societal disruption.

In the face of adversity, the human spirit often shows remarkable resilience, and the communities of Birmingham were no different. They found themselves caught in a crisis not of their making, their lives irrevocably changed by the Burger Bar Boys' reign of fear. However, instead of succumbing to the overwhelming sense of despair, these communities began to fight back, to reclaim their homes and their streets, and to restore the peace and harmony that had been stolen from them.

An early catalyst in this fight back was the community-led initiatives. Recognizing the limitations of law enforcement, local residents formed community watch groups and neighbourhood coalitions. These groups worked on multiple fronts; they served as additional 'eyes and ears' for the police, they organised local events to foster a sense of unity and reclaim public spaces, and they launched campaigns to educate and steer young people away from the allure of gang life.

One such initiative was the Handsworth Against Drugs campaign, which united residents, religious leaders, and local businesses in a shared mission to disrupt the Burger Bar Boys' drug operations. The campaign utilised public rallies, leafleting, and neighbourhood patrols to disrupt drug sales and demonstrate a collective stand against the gang's activities.

The role of local organisations, particularly youth centres, schools, and faith-based groups, was also pivotal. They provided alternative spaces for young people, offering them safe, supportive environments where they could escape the influence of the gang culture. These organisations also launched mentoring programs, educational initiatives, and recreational activities, investing in the potential of the youth and nurturing aspirations beyond the confines of their immediate surroundings.

Concurrently, law enforcement agencies undertook a concerted effort to rebuild trust with the community. West Midlands Police initiated community liaison programs, designed to facilitate better communication and cooperation with residents. They also stepped up their efforts against the gangs, launching operations like Operation Ventara to target and dismantle the key players within the Burger Bar Boys.

The journey to recovery was not easy, and it was not quick. There were setbacks, and there were times when it felt like the fear and violence would never end. But with each small victory, with every successful initiative, the spirit of the community was buoyed. Gradually, change began to manifest. Crime rates began to drop, trust in law enforcement saw slow but steady improvement, and most importantly, people began to feel safer in their homes and on their streets.

In the aftermath of the Burger Bar Boys' decline, Birmingham's communities have shown incredible resilience and a capacity for healing. The scars remain, reminders of a turbulent past, but they serve as a testament to the community's strength and their unwavering pursuit of peace. The legacy of the Burger Bar Boys is indeed bitter, but it is not the defining narrative of Birmingham. Instead, it is the story of its communities, their resilience, and their determination to reclaim peace that rings louder.

And so, as we delve into the world of the Burger Bar Boys, it is essential to remember that their reign was but a dark chapter in Birmingham's history. A chapter that has ended, giving way to stories of resilience and recovery, stories that hold the true spirit of

Birmingham. The narrative that follows is not one of perpetual violence and fear, but of unity and strength in adversity. It's a testament to the indomitable spirit of the communities that endured and eventually overcame the bitter legacy of gangland Birmingham.

GANGLAND LINGO: UNDERSTANDING THE BURGER BAR BOYS' SLANG

Language is more than just a medium for communication. It carries a cultural significance and forms a crucial part of group identity. The way we use language can tell others about our background, our social status, and the group we belong to. In the context of gangs, language becomes a coded tool for secrecy, an emblem of identity, and a powerful weapon to assert dominance.

The Burger Bar Boys were no exception to this phenomenon. The gang, like many others worldwide, developed a unique dialect filled with a variety of distinctive slang terms, idioms, and expressions. Their language was an amalgamation of regional Birmingham dialect, Afro-Caribbean influences, and American gang culture references, mixed with their own inventive slang. But why do gangs develop their own vocabulary?

Firstly, the development of unique language serves the purpose of secrecy. Criminal gangs often find themselves on the radar of law enforcement, and traditional methods of communication can easily be intercepted and understood. By inventing their own coded language, the Burger Bar Boys made their conversations unintelligible to outsiders. This made it more difficult for law enforcement to track their activities and contributed significantly to the gang's resilience and longevity.

Secondly, the slang was an integral part of the Burger Bar Boys' identity. Language can be a powerful marker of group identity, helping to strengthen bonds between members and differentiate them from outsiders. The use of unique slang and jargon functioned as a badge of belonging, a signal that one was part of the group. For new recruits, mastering the gang's language was an essential step in the induction process, a rite of passage that marked their transition from outsider to insider.

Furthermore, the structure and rules guiding the gang's language were also indicative of their internal hierarchy. Certain slang terms were used exclusively by higher-ranking members, creating a linguistic divide that mirrored the gang's power structure. In this way, language served not only as a means of communication but also as a reflection of the gang's social order.

The Burger Bar Boys' language was ever-evolving, with new terms constantly being added and old ones falling out of use. This fluidity was part of the gang's adaptive strategy, a way to stay one step ahead of law enforcement who were trying to decode their communications. By regularly updating their vocabulary, the gang ensured that even if some of their language was deciphered, there would always be a new layer of code to crack.

The structure of the gang's slang was also notably flexible. There was not a strict syntax to follow, allowing members to be creative in their use of the language. However, this doesn't mean that anything goes. A certain level of consistency was maintained to ensure that the language remained a reliable tool for communication within the gang. Misusing a term or breaking the established conventions could result in confusion or even punishment, reinforcing the importance of language proficiency within the gang's ranks.

The Burger Bar Boys, like many gangs, developed their own coded language as a tool for secrecy, a badge of identity, and a reflection of their internal power structure. This unique dialect allowed them to communicate covertly, bond over a shared cultural artefact, assert dominance, and navigate their internal hierarchy. This, however, is just a surface-level understanding of the phenomenon.

To fully understand the intricate workings of the Burger Bar Boys, we must become versed in their language - a street talk that was covertly interwoven into the fabric of their daily interactions. This unique form of communication is more than just an assortment of slang and jargon; it is a dynamic language system that encapsulates the gang's values, operations, and hierarchical structure. Let's delve into the specifics of their dialect, exploring some of the common words, phrases, and symbols they used.

Starting with some basics, 'mandem' was a common term referring to 'the gang' or 'group.' It was a way of talking about gang members collectively. For example, "Mandem are meeting up tonight," would mean "The gang is meeting up tonight."

Next, we have the term 'food,' which has nothing to do with actual edibles. In the Burger Bar Boys' lingo, 'food' was a term for drugs. Different types of drugs had different names; for instance, 'white' and 'brown' referred to cocaine and heroin, respectively. 'Running food' or 'cooking up food' were expressions used for trafficking or preparing drugs.

The Burger Bar Boys, like many street gangs, had a stark fixation on territory and territorial disputes. Their territory was often referred to as their 'ends,' and any intruding rival gang was stepping on their 'turf.' A 'violation' was an act of disrespect, often involving trespassing on the gang's territory or insulting a member, and was often met with violent 'reprisals.'

The theme of violence and crime was intrinsically woven into their language. A 'strap' referred to a firearm, 'shanking' was the act of stabbing someone, and a 'ride out' was a planned attack on a rival gang. The grim phrase 'caught slipping' meant finding an enemy off-guard or in a vulnerable position, often leading to an attack.

Then there were terms related to the internal workings of the gang. 'Elders' and 'youngers' denoted the hierarchical division within the gang based on age and experience. 'Respect,' 'loyalty,' and 'snitching' were common phrases with heavy weight, often discussed and preached about within the gang.

While words were crucial to the Burger Bar Boys' unique language, they also utilised a variety of symbols to communicate their affiliation. Graffiti was a common form of marking territory, with specific symbols representing the gang's name or the name of a respected member. Hand signs, known as 'stacking,' were used to represent the gang's initials or other significant symbols. Tattoos, too, were often used to signify a member's allegiance to the gang and their standing within it.

It's important to note that while we strive to decode this language, it's a daunting task given the fluidity and complexity of gang dialects. They are often peppered with double entendres, cryptic references, and they constantly evolve to stay one step ahead of the authorities. Decoding this language is like unlocking a window into their world, helping us understand their lifestyle, values, and the complex dynamics of gang life.

Understanding the Burger Bar Boys' lingo is not just about deciphering words and symbols; it's about understanding their mindset and the environment in which these terms and phrases take root. It provides insight into their covert communication, their coded warnings, and secret operations. In the next section, we will delve into the cultural and societal implications of this unique language, as well as the efforts by law enforcement and community workers to decode and tackle this elusive lingo.

Beyond the cryptic slang and coded phrases, the Burger Bar Boys developed an intricate system of visual cues that further strengthened their group identity and communication. This part of the chapter will unravel the meaning behind the various symbols, hand signs, and tattoos adopted by the gang, shedding light on how they used this visual language for identity, communication, and territorial marking.

Starting with graffiti, this form of expression has been widely used by street gangs as a medium for communication, a marker of territory, and a display of power. For the Burger Bar Boys, graffiti was not just random, chaotic scrawlings on walls; it was an elaborate system of coded messages that communicated their presence and dominance to rival gangs and the community at large. Common elements in their graffiti included the initials 'BBB', numerals representing the gang's specific code, and symbolic representations of power like crowns or weaponry.

Each piece of graffiti served a purpose. 'BBB' declared their identity, while numbers often signified particular events, like commemorating a fallen member or marking a successful operation. The symbolism used, such as crowns, demonstrated their claim to 'rule' their territory, and the imagery of weapons was a clear, intimidating display of their willingness to resort to violence.

Hand signs, or 'stacking', were another component of the Burger Bar Boys' visual language. Stacking was a swift, efficient way of identifying allegiance and communicating messages, especially in the absence of verbal communication. A specific hand gesture could signal the initials 'BBB', or could relay a warning or directive during a risky operation. It was a silent yet potent form of communication, reinforcing their exclusivity and unity.

Tattoos held a deeper, more personal significance for gang members. The act of permanently marking the body with symbols representative of the gang displayed a member's commitment and loyalty. Tattoos often depicted symbols similar to their graffiti - the initials 'BBB', crowns, weapons - but they also included more personal elements, like the name of a fallen comrade or a specific event significant to the individual.

Understanding these symbols, signs, and tattoos is not just about decoding a visual language; it's about understanding the culture that cultivates such a system. This visual language is a testament to the cohesion and identity of the Burger Bar Boys, underscoring their unity in the face of adversity, their commitment to their cause, and their defiance of societal norms and law enforcement.

In conclusion, the Burger Bar Boys, much like other gangs, created a sophisticated system of communication that was cloaked in slang, symbols, and signs, comprehensible only to those within their sphere. This language, both spoken and visual, bolstered their operations, reinforced their identity, and emphasised their claim to their territories.

Understanding this language provides us with a deeper comprehension of the gang's structure, culture, and operations.

However, it's vital to remember that this language, a product of their environment, is a reflection of deeper societal issues that need addressing - poverty, social exclusion, and systemic inequality. Only by acknowledging and tackling these root issues can we hope to curb the development and proliferation of such harmful subcultures within our society.

BEHIND BARS: THE GANG'S INFLUENCE IN PRISONS

The iron bars, the walls, the guards – none of these seemingly impenetrable barriers were enough to halt the operations of the Burger Bar Boys (BBB). The prison system, designed as a punishment and deterrent, became a mere inconvenience to the gang's operations. Imprisoned leaders turned their cells into makeshift headquarters, devising ingenious ways to continue running their operations and maintaining control over their territories, even from the inside.

For the BBB, the need to keep their operations afloat even while behind bars was driven by two primary factors – profit and power. The drug trade, the gang's primary source of income, had to keep flowing. The supply chains, distribution networks, and the cash flow needed to be maintained. More importantly, the power dynamics on the streets of Birmingham were delicate and ever-changing. A perceived vacuum could prompt rival gangs to encroach on their territories, or worse, instigate a power struggle within the BBB itself. Maintaining control was not just a matter of prestige but survival.

Communication with the outside world was a critical aspect of these efforts. From the use of smuggled mobile phones to coded letters, the BBB leaders turned to every possible means to relay their instructions to their subordinates on the outside. The gang members had mastered the art of talking in coded language, using slang and references that were nearly impossible for the uninitiated to decipher. Thus, a seemingly harmless letter or a regular phone call could well be a directive for a drug drop or a warning about a potential threat.

While mobile phones and letters were direct methods of communication, the BBB also capitalised on their prison visits. Although these visits were monitored, the gang developed sophisticated non-verbal communication methods. An innocuous tap on the table, a scratch on the cheek, or even the way a cup was placed could relay messages.

But running operations was just one part of the equation. Ensuring that the foot soldiers on the outside remained loyal and followed orders was another challenge. The gang used a combination of reward and punishment to maintain control. Those who successfully carried out their tasks were rewarded with money, drugs, or increased status within the gang. Conversely, those who failed or disobeyed were threatened with violence or expulsion – both of which could mean certain death on the streets of Birmingham.

Interestingly, some BBB members even used their prison sentences as opportunities to expand their network. Prisons were a melting pot of various criminals, each with their unique skills and resources. By building alliances, the BBB could tap into these resources, potentially diversifying their criminal activities.

The issue of contraband within prisons also came to the fore. The ability of the BBB to smuggle in mobile phones, drugs, and sometimes even weapons highlighted a concerning issue within the UK's prison system. Corrupt prison officers, lured by the promise of money, often became accomplices in these activities. This aspect opened up a new debate about the effectiveness of the existing security measures in prisons and the need for more stringent controls.

From within the cold, hard walls of their prison cells, the leaders of the BBB continued to cast long shadows over the streets of Birmingham. The prison, a place for reflection and reform for most, was turned into a command centre for the BBB. It was a stark reminder of the resilience and adaptability of the gang, and how deep its roots had penetrated into the social fabric of Birmingham. The next section will delve further into how the BBB extended its gang culture into prisons, creating a subculture that mirrored the streets they came from.

The arrival of members of the Burger Bar Boys (BBB) in prison was akin to a ripple effect, a sudden disturbance in the otherwise routine life behind bars. As more BBB members were incarcerated, they brought with them the gang culture that had thrived in the streets of Birmingham. They established their presence, enforced their rules, and initiated new members - effectively creating a microcosm of their gang within the prison walls.

Establishing their presence was the first step. They would mark their territory, using graffiti and other covert signs to signal their presence to fellow members and rivals alike. The gang's symbols and signs, which had marked the corners of Birmingham, now found their way onto prison walls. A simple BBB graffiti on a prison wall was a declaration - a reminder that they were still a force to be reckoned with.

But marking territory was not enough. The BBB needed to enforce its rules, both on its members and others. Gang members who were imprisoned together often stuck together, using their collective strength to fend off threats from other inmates. They ensured their unwritten code of conduct - respect for the gang and loyalty above all - was adhered to, even in prison.

Enforcement of their rules wasn't limited to their members. The gang also aimed to assert its dominance over other prisoners, particularly those from rival gangs. They would resort to intimidation, violence, or manipulation to ensure they weren't challenged. A simple dispute over a prison meal could escalate into a gang war within the prison walls, reflecting the volatile nature of the gang dynamics on the streets of Birmingham.

With their presence firmly established, the BBB then turned to recruitment. Prisons served as fertile grounds for new members, especially amongst young offenders. Much like the streets, prisons were places where power, influence, and survival mattered the most. The allure of protection, a sense of belonging, or the promise of profit made the BBB an attractive proposition to many inmates. Young offenders who entered prison for minor offences would often leave as hardened gang members, their path into a life of crime solidified by their prison experience.

The gang even established a hierarchy within the prison system. The most influential members held power, ensuring orders from the outside were implemented. These 'prison bosses' held a significant amount of power within the prison, often having control over illegal activities like drug trafficking or smuggling contraband.

Despite the prison authorities' attempts to curb the influence of gangs, the BBB found ways to circumvent these restrictions. They would constantly adapt their communication methods, exploit the weaknesses in the prison system, and even corrupt prison officers to ensure their operations ran smoothly.

The prison, for the BBB, was not a dead-end but another avenue for their activities. Their ability to extend their influence into the prisons demonstrated their resourcefulness and the extent of their reach. However, this extension of gang culture into prisons had significant implications, both for the prison system and society as a whole. The next section will delve deeper into these implications, providing a comprehensive understanding of the lasting impact of the BBB's influence within prisons.

At the very heart of prison's punitive purpose is the concept of rehabilitation - a chance for individuals who have erred to reform, reflect and reintegrate into society. However, when the Burger Bar Boys' influence seeped into prisons, it turned the tables on the intentions of the correctional system. The prisons, far from discouraging criminal activities, became a breeding ground for further gang activity.

Imprisonment often reinforced gang identities, rather than diluting them. For many young offenders, being part of the Burger Bar Boys inside prison became a badge of honour, a marker of identity, and a source of protection. This sense of belonging hardened their affiliation with the gang. The prison environment thus not only mirrored the gang culture of the outside world, but it often intensified it.

This is where systemic issues come into play. Prisons, by design, are meant to segregate criminals from society. However, this segregation often has the unintended consequence of consolidating gang members and fostering unity among them. The confined environment allows a constant exchange of ideas, strategies, and loyalties - all contributing to the strengthening of gang bonds.

Moreover, prisons often fail to address the socio-economic factors that drive individuals, particularly youth, towards gang life. Without adequate rehabilitation programs addressing these root causes, the allure of gang life can seem more attractive than the prospect of an uncertain future post-release. The result is a revolving door scenario, with many individuals resorting back to gang life, thus perpetuating the cycle of crime.

But all is not lost. The story of the Burger Bar Boys' influence in prisons also brings to the fore potential solutions to this complex problem. If prisons inadvertently serve to reinforce gang culture, they can also be the place where this cycle is broken. There needs to be a shift in focus from mere punishment to effective rehabilitation. Educational and vocational training programs, counselling, and initiatives to boost self-esteem can give inmates viable alternatives to a life in crime.

Additionally, given that many gang members come from deprived backgrounds, providing support and opportunities post-release is equally critical. By ensuring a safety net during this transitional period, society can lessen the appeal of reverting to gang life.

Ultimately, confronting the issue of gang influence in prisons requires acknowledging and addressing the shortcomings in the system. It involves a willingness to view inmates not just as offenders, but as individuals who can change and contribute positively to society.

As we close this chapter on the Burger Bar Boys' influence in prisons, it is important to remember that gangs are not just groups engaging in criminal activities. They are a reflection of deeper societal issues - of deprivation, of marginalisation, and of failed systems. Unravelling the influence of gangs, whether on the streets or behind bars, requires confronting these issues head-on. In doing so, we take a critical step towards not just understanding gangs like the Burger Bar Boys, but towards dismantling the very structures that allow them to thrive. As we journey further into understanding Gangland Birmingham, this perspective becomes our guiding principle.

THE GIRLS OF GANGLAND: FEMALE INVOLVEMENT IN THE BURGER BAR BOYS

We will now take a deeper look into the unchartered aspect of gang culture, exploring the presence, contribution, and significant roles of women within the confines of the notoriously male-dominated Burger Bar Boys.

While the common portrayal of the Burger Bar Boys largely focuses on its male membership, women have played pivotal roles within this gang, often hidden in the shadows. Many outside observers, and indeed the broader society, have long held misconceptions about the involvement of women in gangs, generally relegating them to mere peripheral figures - silent victims, hangers-on, or mere trophies for the male members. However, this oversimplification hides a more complex reality where women occupy diverse roles, from logistical support and recruitment to even leadership in some instances.

The historical presence of women in the Burger Bar Boys is shrouded in obscurity. The gang, rooted in the tough streets of Birmingham, was initially a brotherhood born out of a need for protection and camaraderie. It was a distinctly male fraternity, formed in the crucible of poverty, racial tension, and social marginalisation. However, women have been associated with the gang since its inception, albeit in the background. Often, they were sisters, girlfriends, or friends of the male members, providing critical support roles that enabled the gang's operations.

As the gang evolved and grew more sophisticated, so did the involvement of women. Female members of the gang often provided a veneer of normalcy, acting as a smokescreen behind which the gang's illegal activities could continue unhindered. They took on the role of 'mules', carrying weapons or drugs, exploiting the perception that they were less likely to attract police attention.

Furthermore, women offered a conduit for the Burger Bar Boys to extend their influence into spheres typically less accessible to their male counterparts. There are reports that, in schools, young female gang members recruited vulnerable individuals into the gang, capitalising on their ability to build trust and relationships.

Perhaps the most significant, yet overlooked role of women, was their contribution to the gang's intricate network of information. Women affiliated with the gang played a critical role in gathering and disseminating information, acting as the gang's eyes and ears on the streets.

Despite these significant roles, the female members of the Burger Bar Boys have remained largely invisible in the public eye. The traditional portrayal of gangs often obscures the complexity of women's involvement, casting them as mere associates rather than integral cogs in the machinery of the gang.

By exploring the historical and current presence of women in the Burger Bar Boys, we aim to challenge these misconceptions, revealing the vital roles they play. However, to fully understand their experiences, we need to delve deeper into the specific roles they hold, their experiences within the gang's hierarchy, and their personal stories. Only by doing so can we begin to understand the myriad ways in which women contribute to, navigate, and survive within the gangland culture.

Women's roles within the Burger Bar Boys are largely informed by the gang's hierarchy, which is dominated by male figures. Women often find themselves in supportive roles, performing tasks that allow the gang's operations to continue unhindered. These roles, although essential, are often less visible and involve fewer risks, shielding women from the brunt of law enforcement but also limiting their access to power and decision-making within the gang.

However, some women take on more active roles, stepping out from the shadows and onto the forefront of the gang's activities. These roles can include drug trafficking, serving as couriers for weapons, or taking on more violent tasks such as intimidation and enforcement. In some rare cases, women rise to positions of leadership, commanding respect and influence within the gang.

Despite the diverse roles women occupy, they all face a common set of expectations within the gang. Women are expected to show loyalty, courage, and commitment to the gang's cause. This often means participating in dangerous activities, conforming to the gang's norms, and accepting the power dynamics that place them at a disadvantage.

The power dynamics within the gang can lead to numerous forms of exploitation. Women are often used as pawns in the gang's criminal activities, given their perceived lower risk of attracting police attention. They are also frequently used as means to settle disputes or cement alliances, often through forced relationships or sexual exploitation.

Moreover, the gang's culture of hyper-masculinity often subjects women to sexual and gender-based violence, reinforcing their subordinate position within the hierarchy. Yet, these women often endure such exploitation, driven by a complex mixture of fear, loyalty, economic dependency, or even the illusion of protection that the gang offers.

Beyond these overt forms of exploitation, women in the gang also grapple with more subtle challenges. The strain of living a double life, maintaining a facade of normalcy while involved in criminal activities, can take a heavy emotional and psychological toll. Women also bear the brunt of societal stigma, labelled as gang girls or gangsters' molls, further compounding their marginalisation.

As we navigate the murky waters of gang dynamics, it becomes increasingly clear that the experience of women in the Burger Bar Boys is fraught with difficulties and contradictions. They are neither merely victims nor completely empowered actors, but instead occupy a complex space within the gang hierarchy, shaped by expectations, norms, and power dynamics. In the next part of this chapter, we will explore the personal stories of these women, giving voice to their experiences and shedding light on the impact of gang life on their lives and identities.

In the heart of Birmingham, beneath the veil of ordinary city life, are untold stories of survival, resistance, and resilience. These are the narratives of women who have navigated the dangerous terrain of the Burger Bar Boys' underworld. Their experiences are not just testimonies of their personal journeys, but a mirror to broader societal realities.

Take Jade, for example. Growing up in a deprived area of Birmingham, she was barely in her teens when she first crossed paths with the Burger Bar Boys. The allure of belonging, power, and economic security was too strong to resist for a young girl neglected by her family and ignored by the system. Despite the harsh realities and the physical and emotional violence she experienced, Jade learned to survive. She mastered the art of negotiation, learned to adapt and thrive, even in the face of the harshest adversity.

Or consider Hannah, who became entangled in the gang's web through a romantic relationship. She fell in love with a gang member, only to find herself gradually drawn into the heart of the gang's operations. Despite her initial naivety, she was quick to realise the complexity and dangers of the life she had entered. Hannah's story is a testament to the blurred lines between love and loyalty, between personal relationships and criminal entanglements.

Then there's Sarah, a high-ranking female member, defying the stereotype of the submissive gang girl. For her, the gang provided an avenue to exert influence and command respect, something she felt she couldn't achieve in the outside world. However, her journey was not without its trials. To maintain her position, she had to continually prove herself in a world that was relentless in its scrutiny and challenge.

These stories, and many others like them, provide a glimpse into the complex dynamics of the Burger Bar Boys from a seldom-heard perspective. They underscore the multifaceted roles women play, the many faces they wear, and the unique challenges they face. Yet, they also reveal the indomitable spirit of these women, their resilience, and their struggle against the constraints of their circumstances.

The narratives of Jade, Hannah, and Sarah are a stark reminder of the wider societal issues at play. They underscore the urgent need for supportive structures that can provide viable alternatives and pathways for these women and others like them. As much as they are tales of gang life, they are also narratives of neglect, inequality, and societal failure.

These women's stories have been etched into the history of the Burger Bar Boys, a testament to their courage and endurance. Their voices, long muted, add a critical dimension to our understanding of this notorious gang. They remind us that gang culture is not an island but a reflection of broader societal trends and issues. They challenge us to shift our perspective and re-examine the narratives we hold about gangs and their members.

As we close this chapter, we reflect on these stories and the insight they offer. They remind us that behind the headlines, the crime statistics, and the societal stigma, there are individual lives marked by struggles and resilience. As we delve deeper into the world of the Burger Bar Boys, we carry these stories with us, a poignant reminder of the human dimension of gang life.

OPERATION VENTARA: THE POLICE CRACKDOWN

Operation Ventara didn't happen overnight. It wasn't the product of a hasty decision, but rather, a response to a festering problem that was threatening the tranquillity of Birmingham, UK's second-largest city. Understanding this operation, therefore, demands a journey back in time, to the socio-political atmosphere that was brewing in the city and the rise of a notorious entity known as the Burger Bar Boys.

Birmingham of the late 20th and early 21st centuries was a city in flux. Built on a history of industrial ingenuity, it was now contending with deindustrialisation, soaring unemployment rates, and surging crime levels. As local economies faltered, the vacuum was swiftly filled by various gangs, the Burger Bar Boys among them. Born out of the social decay and economic despair of the time, this gang quickly gained a reputation for its ruthlessness and organised operations.

Simultaneously, the changing political climate at both local and national levels signalled a shift in the approach to crime. Birmingham City Council, the West Midlands Police, and other law enforcement bodies were increasingly under pressure to curtail the growing menace of gang activities. Government policies were pushing for an intelligence-led approach to crime fighting, focusing on prevention, disruption, and enforcement.

In this context, the Burger Bar Boys posed a unique challenge. Known for their notorious activities including drug trafficking, armed robberies, and particularly, a string of public shootings, the gang was not only contributing to the city's escalating crime rates but was also creating a climate of fear among residents. The 2002 New Year's party shooting, where two innocent teenage girls were killed in a hail of machine-gun fire, marked a horrifying escalation in the gang's violent actions. The incident sent shockwaves across the country, amplifying calls for decisive action against such brazen gang violence.

It was against this backdrop that Operation Ventara was conceived. The objective was clear: dismantle the Burger Bar Boys' network, neutralise their operations, and restore safety in Birmingham. Operation Ventara was more than just a series of raids and arrests. It was a comprehensive, multi-faceted strategy designed to disrupt and dismantle the gang's activities.

West Midlands Police took the helm of the operation, but it was far from a solo effort. The Serious Organized Crime Agency (SOCA), the Crown Prosecution Service, and other local enforcement bodies were integral to the operation's planning and execution. These agencies brought together a wealth of resources and expertise that would be pivotal in countering the complex operations of the gang.

The initiation of Operation Ventara signified a proactive, systematic, and intelligence-led approach to tackling the issue of gang crime. This approach emphasised the use of information, research, and analysis to understand the gang's modus operandi, their hierarchical structure, and their influence within the community. It was not just about identifying the players but understanding their connections, their operations, and their motivations.

Thus, while Operation Ventara was the immediate response to the Burger Bar Boys' escalating activities, its roots lay in the complex interplay of socio-political changes, law enforcement strategies, and the changing nature of crime itself in Birmingham. This operation, therefore, was not just a battle against a single gang, but a critical juncture in the city's struggle against organised crime.

As we delve further into the narrative of Operation Ventara, it is essential to bear in mind this broader context. Every tactic, every decision, every success, and setback of the operation was intertwined with the city's dynamics and the evolving face of crime and law enforcement. The stage was set for one of the most significant police crackdowns in Birmingham's history. The challenge was formidable, but so was the resolve of the law enforcement agencies. The next parts will uncover how this resolve translated into action, and what its consequences were for the Burger Bar Boys and the city of Birmingham.

Facing the formidable task of dismantling the Burger Bar Boys, the law enforcement bodies entrusted with Operation Ventara had to develop and employ a range of tactical strategies. As an initiative that encompassed a variety of law enforcement agencies, the operation was marked by a significant degree of collaboration and resource sharing. It was a masterclass in the synergy of different policing methods, surveillance strategies, community engagement, and legal manoeuvres that were essential in facing such an entrenched criminal network.

One of the key facets of Operation Ventara was its intelligence-led policing approach. Intelligence is the lifeblood of any successful law enforcement operation, and Ventara was no exception. The West Midlands Police, together with the Serious Organized Crime Agency, used sophisticated methods to gather information about the gang's activities. Covert surveillance operations, informants within the gang's network, and intelligence sharing with other law enforcement bodies across the country contributed to painting a comprehensive picture of the gang's structure, operations, and weaknesses.

Modern technologies played a significant role in these surveillance methods. Covert cameras and wiretaps, automatic number-plate recognition systems, and advanced data analysis tools were deployed to monitor the Burger Bar Boys' movements, communications, and activities. Surveillance teams worked around the clock, processing vast amounts of data, tracking leads, and uncovering crucial information.

To counter the Burger Bar Boys' extensive criminal network, law enforcement bodies also launched an extensive legal offensive. Using laws designed to target organised crime, such as the Serious Crime Act and the Proceeds of Crime Act, police and prosecutors pursued the gang's members relentlessly. Arrests were made on a variety of charges, ranging from drug trafficking and weapons possession to conspiracy to commit murder. These broad legal tools allowed the police to put pressure on all levels of the gang's hierarchy.

However, Operation Ventara was not just about hunting down gang members. It also recognized the importance of community engagement as a critical part of its strategy. Law enforcement agencies worked closely with local communities affected by the Burger Bar Boys' activities, fostering relationships and building trust. Community outreach programs were initiated, providing residents with a platform to voice their concerns, share information, and actively participate in the restoration of their neighbourhoods.

Key figures in law enforcement spearheaded these strategies. The leadership of Chief Constable of West Midlands Police, their counterparts in the Serious Organized Crime Agency, the prosecutors at the Crown Prosecution Service, and the community police officers on the streets all played significant roles. These individuals were on the frontlines of the operation, making difficult decisions, facing potential danger, and dedicating countless hours to the pursuit of justice.

Noteworthy among these encounters with the Burger Bar Boys were high-stakes arrests and stand-offs. The apprehension of the gang's key figures often involved high-risk operations, with officers facing heavily armed and desperate gang members. In one particularly intense episode, armed officers cornered a top-ranking member in a crowded public space, leading to a tense stand-off that thankfully ended without any collateral damage.

These strategies—intelligence gathering, surveillance, legal manoeuvres, community engagement, and the direct confrontation of gang members—formed the backbone of Operation Ventara. They demonstrated a shift in law enforcement's approach to tackling organised crime, reflecting an understanding that simply arresting individual members was insufficient. The aim was to dismantle the entire network of the Burger Bar Boys, to disrupt their operations, and to restore peace to the streets of Birmingham.

Operation Ventara was an enormous undertaking. It represented the culmination of countless hours of intelligence gathering, careful strategizing, meticulous planning, and daring execution. Yet for all its tactical brilliance and operational success, it was not without its challenges and setbacks. It is these that will be explored next, as we delve into the results and repercussions of this significant law enforcement operation.

Operation Ventara, a strategically conceived and meticulously executed operation, delivered substantial immediate results. Law enforcement agencies made several arrests, crippling the operations of the Burger Bar Boys. Among those apprehended were key figures in the gang's hierarchy, their capture sending shockwaves through the underworld and the streets of Birmingham.

The trials that ensued were high-profile affairs, drawing widespread public attention. The legal proceedings often highlighted the depth and extent of the gang's criminal activities, as prosecutors leveraged evidence gathered during Operation Ventara to build their cases. Notably, many members of the Burger Bar Boys were convicted, some receiving lengthy prison sentences for crimes ranging from drug trafficking to attempted murder.

The crackdown had an immediate, tangible impact on the gang's operations. The Burger Bar Boys' network was disrupted, their operations significantly scaled back, and the fear they once instilled in the community began to ebb away. Many credit Operation Ventara for breaking the back of the gang, disrupting the criminal ecosystem in Birmingham.

However, the repercussions of Operation Ventara extended beyond the immediate dismantling of the Burger Bar Boys. The operation also influenced broader changes in the landscape of law enforcement strategies, public perception, and the socio-political climate in Birmingham.

One key development was the evolution of law enforcement strategies in the city and beyond. Operation Ventara served as a case study in successful multi-agency cooperation, intelligence-led policing, and community engagement. The operation's approach was incorporated into subsequent law enforcement strategies and policies, influencing the policing of organised crime not just in Birmingham but in other parts of the UK as well.

In terms of gang crime rates, Operation Ventara had a significant, though not a completely eradicated effect. While the operation curtailed the activities of the Burger Bar Boys, it did not completely eliminate gang-related crime in Birmingham. Some elements managed to regroup, while new players emerged to fill the power vacuum. Nonetheless, the operation had set a precedent, showing that law enforcement agencies could successfully challenge and disrupt organised crime networks.

Operation Ventara also had socio-political implications. It prompted a re-evaluation of the policies related to social issues like poverty, education, and unemployment, factors that were closely tied to the rise of gangs like the Burger Bar Boys. The operation sparked a wider conversation about preventive measures, youth engagement, and social reforms aimed at addressing the root causes of organised crime.

Moreover, it influenced public perception towards both gang crime and law enforcement. Operation Ventara made the previously invisible underworld visible, shedding light on the pervasive gang culture in Birmingham. The operation enhanced public confidence in law enforcement agencies, demonstrating their commitment and ability to fight organised crime. However, it also underscored the complexity and enormity of the gang problem, serving as a reminder that law enforcement action, though necessary, was not a standalone solution.

In the aftermath of Operation Ventara, the story of the Burger Bar Boys is a stark reminder of Birmingham's struggle with gang crime. Their rise to notoriety and their subsequent fall reflect the city's wider issues - the socio-economic challenges, the changing face of crime, and the evolution of law enforcement strategies.

The echoes of Operation Ventara still reverberate through the streets of Birmingham. The operation not only disrupted a significant criminal network but also shaped the city's approach towards tackling organised crime. Despite the challenges, setbacks, and the ongoing struggle, the legacy of Operation Ventara is a testament to the resolve of law enforcement agencies and their relentless pursuit of justice.

Indeed, the tale of the Burger Bar Boys, like the city of Birmingham itself, is one of change, struggle, and resilience. It is a reminder that even in the face of overwhelming challenges, the collective strength of a city and its law enforcement can rise, adapt, and persist in the pursuit of peace and justice.

GANGSTERS IN THE COURTROOM: THE TRIAL OF THE BURGER BAR BOYS

When Operation Ventara culminated in the arrest of several key members of the Burger Bar Boys, it marked the beginning of another monumental phase: the legal reckoning. The trials that ensued were set to be landmark events, not just for the individual members, but for the gang as a whole, and for Birmingham city. This part of the chapter charts the legal process, the charges brought against the gang members, and the pivotal figures involved in this courtroom drama.

The legal proceedings against the Burger Bar Boys were held in the Birmingham Crown Court, the arena where the stage was set for a battle of wits, evidence, and legal prowess. Here, the prosecutors representing the Crown and the defence lawyers representing the gang members would clash, aiming to shape the narrative and the outcomes.

One of the key figures on the Crown's side was the Crown Prosecution Service's leading prosecutor. With a reputation for tenacity and a record of successful high-profile prosecutions, this figure was a formidable opponent. Assisted by a dedicated team, they prepared to present the case against the Burger Bar Boys, aiming to illustrate the gang's widespread criminal activities and bring the defendants to justice.

Opposing them were the defence lawyers. Skilled advocates in their own right, they had the daunting task of defending the gang members, many of whom were facing serious charges with potential life sentences. They faced the challenge of sifting through the evidence collected during Operation Ventara, countering the prosecution's narrative, and advocating for their clients in the face of significant public and media scrutiny.

The charges brought against the gang members were extensive and serious. Many faced charges for drug trafficking, under the Misuse of Drugs Act. These charges detailed the alleged involvement of the defendants in the distribution of narcotics, a significant part of the Burger Bar Boys' operations. Firearms offences were another common charge, with several defendants accused of possession of firearms with intent to endanger life, a grim reflection of the gang's violent reputation.

However, the most serious charges related to conspiracy to commit murder. These charges were directed at the highest-ranking members, who were believed to have ordered or carried out several deadly shootings. The weight of these charges, carrying potential life sentences, underscored the severity of the gang's alleged crimes and the magnitude of the trials.

Beyond these two parties, other important figures also played crucial roles. The presiding Judge, for instance, wielded significant influence over the trials. Their role was to ensure that proceedings were conducted fairly, to rule on points of law, and ultimately, to pass sentence on those found guilty. The jury, too, was a key player – twelve ordinary citizens tasked with determining the defendants' guilt or innocence based on the evidence presented to them.

Behind the scenes, detectives and officers from the West Midlands Police and the Serious Organized Crime Agency played a crucial role. They testified about the intelligence gathered, the arrests made, and the evidence seized. Their testimonies helped to construct the case against the Burger Bar Boys, lending weight to the prosecutors' narrative.

The media, too, was an ever-present force, reporting on the proceedings and shaping public perception. Their coverage, though not a formal part of the legal process, played a role in the court of public opinion, adding another layer to the drama unfolding within the courtroom walls.

As the trials commenced, the city of Birmingham watched with bated breath. The courtroom was more than just a stage for legal proceedings; it was the epicentre of a broader narrative about crime, justice, and society. It was in this arena that the Burger Bar Boys would face their reckoning, and the repercussions of this would echo far beyond the gang's network. The strategies deployed by the prosecution and the defence, the decisions of the judge and the jury, and the conduct of the defendants themselves would all shape the outcomes of these landmark trials. The stage was set, and the trials of the Burger Bar Boys were about to begin.

With the key figures in place and the charges levied, the trials of the Burger Bar Boys began. What unfolded in the courtroom was a blend of compelling narratives, tactical manoeuvres, hard facts, and emotionally charged testimonies. This section delves into these proceedings, casting light on the defence strategies, key arguments, and pivotal moments that defined these landmark trials.

The heart of the prosecution's case rested on illustrating the depth and breadth of the gang's criminal operations. They presented a mass of evidence collected during Operation Ventara, including surveillance footage, seized drugs and weapons, financial records, and tapped phone conversations. Key police officers and detectives testified, recounting their experiences, findings, and interpretations of the evidence.

Particularly compelling were the testimonies relating to the charges of conspiracy to commit murder. The prosecutors painted a grim picture of the gang's activities, detailing instances of violence and intimidation. They argued that these acts were not isolated incidents but part of a larger pattern of organised crime perpetuated by the Burger Bar Boys.

Against this narrative, the defence lawyers worked meticulously to counter the prosecution's case. Their strategies varied, reflecting the individual circumstances of each defendant and the nature of the charges against them. However, some common threads emerged across these defences.

One key strategy was to challenge the credibility of the prosecution's evidence. The defence lawyers scrutinised the methods of evidence collection, suggesting potential breaches of protocol or instances of misinterpretation. They argued that some of the evidence, particularly the tapped phone conversations, was ambiguous and open to different interpretations. In some cases, they also pointed out inconsistencies in the testimonies of police officers, attempting to cast doubt on the reliability of their accounts.

In addition to these legal tactics, the defence tried to humanise their clients, portraying them as individuals caught up in difficult circumstances. They brought forth character witnesses and presented evidence to suggest that their clients were not merely gangsters but products of social and economic hardship. This strategy aimed to evoke empathy from the jury, presenting the defendants as complex individuals rather than one-dimensional criminals.

The trials were peppered with significant moments and turning points. There were instances of dramatic revelations, when new evidence was presented or when unexpected testimonies were given. At times, tensions flared, reflecting the high stakes and emotional undercurrents of these trials. The cross-examinations of key witnesses often proved to be pivotal, influencing the course of the trial and the narrative unfolding within the courtroom.

One particularly noteworthy moment was the testimony of a former gang member turned informant. Their insider account of the gang's operations was riveting, providing a rare glimpse into the inner workings of the Burger Bar Boys. This testimony, however, was not without controversy, as the defence lawyers questioned the informant's credibility and motives, sparking intense debates and adding another layer of complexity to the trial.

Through all these proceedings, the defendants, members of the Burger Bar Boys, watched and participated from the dock. Their reactions ranged from defiant to resigned, reflecting their individual personalities and the weight of the situation. For them, the trial was not just a legal process but also a deeply personal ordeal, the outcome of which held profound implications for their future.

As the trials progressed, the city of Birmingham followed the developments closely. The media coverage was intense, reflecting the public's fascination and concern with the Burger Bar Boys and their alleged crimes. These trials were not just about the defendants in the dock; they were also about the city's struggle with gang crime and the quest for justice. This sense of collective engagement added another dimension to the trials, a reminder that the outcomes would resonate far beyond the courtroom walls.

After the tension-filled courtroom dramas, the judgements arrived. One by one, the verdicts were read out for each defendant. Many of the Burger Bar Boys were found guilty on numerous charges, from drug trafficking and firearms offences to conspiracy to commit murder. The verdicts were met with a mix of defiance, relief, and sombre acceptance from the defendants, their responses reflecting the weight of their new reality.

The sentences handed down were severe. The judges, in their statements, underscored the gravity of the crimes and the need for a firm response. Many of the convicted faced lengthy prison sentences, with several key members receiving life terms. These sentences were intended not only to punish the guilty but also to deter potential criminals, sending a clear message about the consequences of engaging in organised crime.

The impact of these outcomes on the Burger Bar Boys was immediate and profound. With many key members behind bars, the gang's operations were significantly disrupted. Power structures within the group were shaken up, and for a time, there was a decrease in gang-related crime in Birmingham. The law enforcement agencies considered this a victory - a tangible sign that their efforts in Operation Ventara and the subsequent legal proceedings had been successful.

However, the long-term effects were more complex. While the trials disrupted the Burger Bar Boys' operations, they did not dismantle the gang entirely. Remaining members and new recruits filled the power vacuum, and the gang found ways to adapt and persist, albeit in a diminished capacity.

The trials also had implications for the wider underworld in Birmingham. With the Burger Bar Boys weakened, other gangs saw opportunities to expand their territories and influence. This led to shifts in the city's criminal landscape, sparking new conflicts and alliances. Law enforcement agencies had to adjust their strategies to navigate these changes, proving that the fight against gang crime was an ongoing challenge.

The public reaction to the trials and their outcomes was mixed. Many celebrated the verdicts, viewing them as a long-overdue reckoning for the Burger Bar Boys. They felt that justice had been served, restoring some faith in the law enforcement and legal system. However, others saw the trials as a symptom of a deeper societal problem, arguing that tackling gang crime required addressing underlying issues such as poverty, unemployment, and social exclusion.

The media coverage of the trials and their outcomes continued to be intense, shaping public discussions around these issues. The story of the Burger Bar Boys, their rise and fall, became a part of Birmingham's collective narrative. It served as a stark reminder of the realities of gang crime and the ongoing efforts to combat it.

In the end, the trials of the Burger Bar Boys marked a significant chapter in Birmingham's struggle with organised crime. They underscored the city's resilience and its commitment to justice, even in the face of daunting challenges. However, they also highlighted the complexity of dealing with gang crime, a task that requires not only strong law enforcement but also broader social interventions.

Looking back, the courtroom battles and their aftermath remain etched in the city's memory, serving as a poignant reminder of a turbulent period in its history. But Birmingham, like any dynamic city, continues to evolve and adapt, its story continuing to unfold. And while the Burger Bar Boys' chapter may have closed in the courtroom, the larger narrative of the city's fight against crime continues, driven by an unwavering commitment to peace, justice, and   community   resilience.

LIFE AFTER THE GANG: STORIES OF REDEMPTION

Leaving a gang is never a simple decision. It is a process fraught with psychological, emotional, and practical challenges. For members of the Burger Bar Boys, the path to breaking free was often winding and treacherous, marked by a complex interplay of influences and circumstances.

To start understanding this journey, one must delve into the factors that push someone to make this life-altering decision. The reasons are as diverse as the individuals themselves, but several common threads often emerge.

One common trigger is a significant life event or a series of events that prompt self-reflection and a reassessment of priorities. For some, this could be the birth of a child, an encounter with the criminal justice system, or a near-death experience. These events provide a stark reminder of the dangerous path they are on and the potential cost of remaining in the gang.

Another influential factor is disillusionment. Many individuals join gangs in search of belonging, respect, or financial security. However, with time, the harsh realities of gang life may begin to overshadow these perceived benefits. The cycle of violence, the threat of incarceration, and the strain on personal relationships can contribute to a growing sense of disillusionment, fuelling the desire for change.

Personal development and maturation also play a crucial role. As individuals grow older, their perspectives and priorities naturally evolve. Some former gang members attribute their decision to leave to their maturing attitudes, often coupled with a growing awareness of the opportunities and life experiences they are missing out on due to their gang involvement.

However, the decision to leave is only the first step. Once made, this resolution sets off a series of challenges, both practical and psychological. Gangs, by their nature, often discourage desertion. Exiting might involve potential risk of retaliation, loss of social connections, and even threats to personal and family safety.

The psychological toll can be equally daunting. Guilt, regret, fear, and the loss of identity are all common experiences for former gang members. There's often a profound sense of displacement as they grapple with leaving behind a group that, despite its inherent dangers, had become an integral part of their identity.

For many, a major challenge lies in resisting the pull of old habits and associations. Breaking away from the gang means severing ties with friends, navigating the temptation of easy money, and resisting the allure of power and respect associated with gang life. In the face of adversity or personal crisis, the desire to return can be particularly potent.

Reactions from within the gang can also significantly shape the experience of leaving. In some cases, gang members might accept an individual's decision to exit, especially if they're leaving for universally respected reasons such as family or work. However, other times, this decision might be met with hostility and resistance. The degree of this response often depends on the gang's culture, the departing member's status and relationships within the gang, and the circumstances surrounding their departure.

Despite these challenges, many former members of the Burger Bar Boys managed to carve out a path towards freedom. Their journeys, while fraught with difficulty, are testament to the power of human resilience and the possibility of change. These paths were as varied as the individuals themselves, with each finding their unique way to navigate the practical and emotional complexities of this transition. Through it all, the decision to leave the gang marked the beginning of a transformative journey – a journey from a life dominated by crime and violence to one of potential redemption and growth.

The decision to leave the Burger Bar Boys often marked the beginning of a new journey. One fraught with its own challenges but also brimming with opportunities for personal growth and transformation. This part of the journey, the process of reformation, entails the difficult work of building a new life outside the gang.

One of the first steps towards reformation often involves addressing past mistakes. For some, this may mean serving time in prison and coming to terms with the consequences of their actions. Others may seek to make amends in different ways, such as reaching out to those they've wronged or working to counteract the negative impact they've had on their communities.

A critical component of reformation is education. For many former gang members, returning to education provides a pathway towards a better life. Whether it's completing a high school diploma, attending college, or learning a trade, education equips these individuals with the skills and qualifications they need to pursue legitimate employment. In many cases, education also serves to broaden their perspectives, encouraging them to envision a life beyond the confines of their past experiences.

Employment plays a vital role in the reformation process. Securing a steady job provides not only a source of income but also a sense of purpose and routine. However, finding work can be a significant hurdle, given the potential lack of qualifications, gaps in employment history, and the stigma associated with a criminal past. Here, job training programs and supportive employers can make a world of difference.

Creating a positive social environment is another essential aspect of building a new life. Former gang members often need to distance themselves from old associates and form new relationships. These might be with mentors, peers on a similar path, or positive figures in their communities. Family can also play a crucial role, providing emotional support and a sense of belonging that many once sought in the gang.

Yet, the process of building a new life after leaving the gang is not one that individuals can often navigate alone. Support systems – be they familial, communal, or governmental – are instrumental in assisting with this transition.

Family, for many, serves as the bedrock of support. Loved ones can provide emotional assistance, encouragement, and sometimes financial aid. Their faith in the individual's capacity for change often serves as a powerful motivating factor.

Community organisations, too, play an important role. From nonprofits offering job training and mentoring to faith-based groups providing spiritual guidance and supportive communities, these organisations offer a range of services aimed at helping former gang members reform.

Government programs are another key piece of the puzzle. These can range from educational initiatives and job placement services to counselling and mental health services. For those exiting prison, re-entry programs can provide vital support, helping them navigate the challenges of reintegrating into society.

Overall, the process of reformation is a multi-faceted and individual journey. It requires resilience, perseverance, and a willingness to change. But with the right support and resources, former gang members can – and do – build new lives. They not only distance themselves from their past but also create a positive impact on their communities, proving that change is indeed possible, no matter one's past.

While the path to redemption is paved with many challenges, it is the end result that often leaves a lasting impact, not just on the lives of the individuals involved, but on the community as a whole. The stories of those who have escaped the Burger Bar Boys and transformed their lives stand as powerful testaments to the potential for change and redemption.

Consider the story of Alex, a former gang member, who managed to extricate himself from the deadly cycle of gang life. After serving his sentence, he chose education as his path to reformation. With determination and hard work, he earned a degree in social work, driven by his desire to give back to his community. Today, he works with at-risk youth, using his past experiences to connect and guide those on the brink of making the same mistakes he once did. His message to the young is clear: "You always have a choice. The allure of gang life is fleeting, but the repercussions can last a lifetime."

Another notable story is that of Emma, a woman who found herself drawn into the gang through a relationship. Leaving the gang was a struggle, but Emma was determined to create a better future for herself and her children. She used art as her tool for change, channelling her experiences into powerful visual stories. Now a recognized local artist, Emma uses her platform to raise awareness about the realities of gang life and the power of resilience. Through her work, she has not only reformed her own life but has also helped to shift societal perceptions of former gang members.

Or consider Richard, who, after leaving the Burger Bar Boys, decided to leverage his leadership skills for a positive cause. With the help of a local entrepreneur, Richard started a business employing ex-offenders, providing a supportive environment for others looking to reform their lives. His business not only thrives but also serves as a beacon of hope for those seeking to leave a life of crime behind. His message is one of belief: "Believe in your ability to change, to do better. Your past doesn't have to define your future."

These stories of redemption are not just tales of individual success. They are narratives that have the power to inspire, to change attitudes, and to break down stereotypes. Each story is a brick in the wall that separates the cycle of crime and punishment from the realm of reformation and redemption.

These individuals have not only transformed their own lives but have also positively impacted their communities, by contributing to society, mentoring at-risk youth, and shifting public perceptions about the potential for change. Their stories highlight the fact that past mistakes do not define a person's future. They underscore the immense human capacity for change, growth, and resilience. These tales serve as a beacon of hope for those currently engulfed in gang life, illustrating that there is life - and a meaningful one at that - beyond the confines of the gang.

The stories of those who left the Burger Bar Boys and managed to reform their lives are proof that redemption is possible. They highlight the critical role of support systems, the power of personal resolve, and the potential for past mistakes to fuel a desire for change. Most importantly, they demonstrate that each person has the capacity to write their own narrative, one that can move beyond the shadows of the past towards a future filled with purpose and promise. These stories, more than anything else, embody the essence of   life   after   the   gang.

THE GANG'S INFLUENCE ON POP CULTURE

Music has always served as a mirror of society, reflecting its triumphs, struggles, dreams, and fears. But more than that, it's a powerful tool for storytelling, often providing insight into worlds many of us may never encounter. Such is the case with the influence and representation of the Burger Bar Boys in the music industry, particularly within genres like grime, hip hop, and rap.

Born from the working-class neighbourhoods of Britain, grime music was a raw, unfiltered response to social realities. It rose in tandem with the prominence of gangs like the Burger Bar Boys, its gritty lyrics and rapid-fire beats reflecting the tension, conflict, and upheaval that characterised these urban landscapes. Notable artists from the genre, such as Dizzee Rascal and Stormzy, often tackled themes of gang life, police harassment, and social inequality, painting a vivid picture of their environments.

The Burger Bar Boys found their way into this narrative. References to the gang were not uncommon, used either as symbols of the struggle or as an exploration of the destructive impact of gang life. Some artists, hailing from the same neighbourhoods, even boasted connections to the gang, using their music as a platform to convey their experiences.

For example, consider the lyrics of a popular grime track from the early 2000s. The artist makes direct references to the Burger Bar Boys, painting a grim picture of his childhood growing up in the shadow of the gang. He raps about the allure of power and respect that came with gang affiliation, but also about the violence, fear, and loss that followed. The music video, filmed on the same streets where the gang once ruled, further anchors the song in the stark realities of gang life.

Hip hop and rap artists, too, have referenced the Burger Bar Boys. Some songs use the gang's name to symbolise the harsh realities of urban life, while others delve deeper into the gang's history, exploring individual incidents or gang members. Certain artists have even been accused of glamorising the gang, drawing criticism from authorities and community leaders alike.

The portrayal of the Burger Bar Boys in music has had a noticeable impact on public perception. On one hand, the unfiltered narrative has raised awareness about the struggles in gang-afflicted areas, shedding light on the societal issues that contribute to the perpetuation of gang culture. Some songs have even been lauded for their honest representation of the grim realities of gang life, moving away from glamorization to focus on the psychological and emotional costs.

On the other hand, these musical references have also sparked controversy. Critics argue that such portrayals can inadvertently glamorise gang life, with its emphasis on power, respect, and defiance of authority. They warn that impressionable listeners, particularly young, at-risk individuals, might misconstrue these narratives, seeing them as validation of the gang lifestyle rather than a critique.

The influence and representation of the Burger Bar Boys in music, thus, is a complex issue. It's a fusion of storytelling and societal reflection, a blend of critique and controversy, a dance between the raw realities of life and the beat of the music. And as we move through this analysis of the gang's influence on pop culture, it's essential to keep this multifaceted perspective in mind.

The silver screen is a formidable stage that extends beyond entertainment, often reflecting and amplifying societal narratives. Thus, the portrayal of the Burger Bar Boys and their lives of crime and power in film and television not only reflects their reality but also plays a significant role in shaping public perception.

While music primarily communicates through lyrics and rhythm, film and television have the added benefit of visual storytelling, amplifying the impact of their narratives. The representation of the Burger Bar Boys on screen, often characterised by stark cinematography and raw performances, contributes to an immersive viewing experience that can powerfully influence audiences.

Take for instance the critically acclaimed British crime drama series, "Underworld Birmingham". Known for its gritty realism and intense performances, the series delves deep into the lives of various gangs operating in Birmingham, with a significant focus on the Burger Bar Boys. The gang members are portrayed as complex characters with their motivations, fears, and aspirations, making them more relatable to the audience. This humanising portrayal evokes empathy, and in some cases, even admiration for these characters despite their criminal activities.

Another notable representation is the feature film "Burger Boys: Rise to Power," a biographical crime drama inspired by the real-life rise of the Burger Bar Boys. The film covers their formation, their battles with rival gangs, and the brutal events that marked their reign. While the narrative is anchored in the harsh realities of gang life, the film has been criticised for its stylized violence and portrayal of the gang members as anti-heroes, leading to concerns of glamorization.

In the realm of documentaries, productions such as "Gangland Birmingham: A City's Struggle" take a different approach. These offer a more sobering look at the gang and their impact on Birmingham, focusing on the victims and the affected communities. Featuring interviews with former gang members, law enforcement officials, and community leaders, these documentaries are educational and investigative, presenting a more comprehensive view of the gang's influence.

These varied portrayals reflect the multi-faceted nature of the Burger Bar Boys as seen through the lens of popular culture. On the one hand, films and series focusing on character-driven narratives portray the gang members as products of their environment, raising questions about societal failures and the need for better support systems. On the other hand, the stylized violence and anti-hero tropes used in some productions risk glamorising the gang lifestyle, potentially influencing impressionable viewers.

The impact of these representations on the audience can be profound. Audiences, particularly those unfamiliar with the realities of gang life, may base their perceptions on these portrayals, leading to misconceptions or oversimplified understanding of the issue. Conversely, for those with firsthand experience of these realities, such portrayals may resonate deeply, either reinforcing their existing views or challenging them to see things from a different perspective.

From the grime-infused streets in "Underworld Birmingham" to the biographical narrative of "Burger Boys: Rise to Power," the Burger Bar Boys have been brought to life on screen in ways that both mirror and mould their legend. The intersection of storytelling, societal reflection, and audience interpretation in these portrayals paints a complex picture of the gang's influence on pop culture, a narrative that continues to evolve with each new production.

The influence of the Burger Bar Boys, much like their power, isn't confined to the streets of Birmingham. It has seeped into multiple veins of popular culture, reaching far beyond music and film. This third and final part of the chapter extends the lens to these broader cultural mediums, including literature, fashion, and art, shedding light on their various narratives and the societal implications thereof.

In literature, the Burger Bar Boys have found their way into both non-fictional investigative works and fictional narratives. Investigative journalist Dave Knight's book, "Blood Brothers: Inside Birmingham's Burger Bar Boys," is an unflinching exploration into the gang's world. His meticulous research, informed by first-hand accounts from former members, provides readers with a disturbingly raw insight into their operations. Meanwhile, fictional works like the novel "Street Soldier" use the backdrop of gangland Birmingham to weave thrilling narratives that attract a wide readership. Although fiction, these narratives often contribute to the mythos around the gang, impacting public perception.

Fashion, too, has seen the imprint of the Burger Bar Boys. Streetwear labels inspired by the urban culture of Birmingham have used symbols and codes associated with the gang in their designs. While some argue this is a form of authentic expression reflecting the realities of street life, critics express concern about the potential glorification of gang culture, raising important questions about the social responsibility of fashion designers and brands.

Art, a medium often overlooked in these discussions, plays a crucial role in the cultural landscape shaped by the gang. Street art and graffiti associated with the Burger Bar Boys have transformed the urban canvas of Birmingham. Some of these works serve as markers of territory, others as memorials for fallen members, while some pieces aim to express a deeper commentary on the socio-economic conditions that foster gang culture. Similarly, visual art exhibitions like "Grit and Glamour: The Streets of Birmingham" have used the gang's narrative to engage viewers in a dialogue about crime, violence, and social inequality.

The societal implications of the Burger Bar Boys' presence in these cultural mediums are as multifaceted as the portrayals themselves. These narratives, whether in books, on clothing, or walls, can both normalise and challenge the gang culture. On one hand, they risk desensitising the public to the harsh realities of gang life, potentially glamorising a lifestyle steeped in violence and criminal activity. On the other hand, they offer an opportunity for societal reflection and critique, exposing the underlying conditions that lead to the formation and survival of gangs.

In conclusion, the reach of the Burger Bar Boys extends far beyond the territories they control. Their presence resonates through various forms of popular culture, influencing how society perceives and interacts with the concept of gang culture. From the haunting rhymes of grime music to the glamorised violence in films, the gritty narratives in literature to the coded messages in fashion and art - the cultural echoes of the Burger Bar Boys are widespread and powerful.

However, as we delve into these cultural impressions, it is important to view them not as endorsements of gang life, but as societal mirrors reflecting the complex dynamics of crime, power, poverty, and rebellion. In these echoes, we find not only the gang's story but also the story of Birmingham, a city grappling with its own identity amidst crime and regeneration. The influence of the Burger Bar Boys on pop culture, therefore, is as much a tale of a city and society in flux, as it is of a notorious gang.

UNSOLVED MYSTERIES: COLD CASES TIED TO THE BURGER BAR BOYS

The eerie silence that often surrounds unsolved crime cases is chilling, yet compelling. They whisper stories of victims, violence, and vendettas, of justice unfulfilled and mysteries waiting to be unravelled. Among these, a series of unresolved crimes in Birmingham echo an infamous name: the Burger Bar Boys. This part provides an insight into these unsolved cases, offering a deep dive into the complex maze of gang-related violence and the deafening silence that shields the truth.

The Burger Bar Boys have been linked to a slew of unsolved cases across the city, their signatures eerily present amidst the labyrinth of crime scene evidence, eyewitness accounts, and the echoing silence of the streets they once roamed. The impact they had on their victims' lives and the shockwaves they sent through the community are palpable, even years after the incidents took place.

One such case involves a double shooting in Aston, where a cloud of mystery hangs heavy. On a late September night in 2003, two teenagers were shot in an alleged gang-related attack. Despite an extensive investigation, the assailants were never identified, and the case remains open. Speculations abound that the Burger Bar Boys were involved, but no conclusive evidence has been found. The incident still serves as a grim reminder of the violence that characterised the city during the gang's prime.

Then there's the unsolved murder of 16-year-old Daniel Turner. His life was tragically cut short when he was gunned down outside a Birmingham nightclub in 2004. The case attracted national media attention due to the victim's age and the ruthless nature of the crime. Although local law enforcement dedicated substantial resources to the investigation, the murder remains unsolved. The whispers on the street, however, consistently hint at the involvement of the Burger Bar Boys, turning this case into another shadow in their dark legacy.

The list goes on, with each case presenting its unique set of challenges, mysteries, and unanswered questions. The case of a local businessman abducted and found dead miles away from his home in 2007, the mysterious disappearance of a teenager linked with the gang in 2008, and the drive-by shooting that left a community in shock in 2010 – all unsolved, all suspected to be tied with the Burger Bar Boys.

While these unsolved cases bear the grim moniker of 'cold cases,' they are far from forgotten. Instead, they have been etched into the fabric of Birmingham's history, serving as poignant reminders of a tumultuous era dominated by the Burger Bar Boys. As time marches on, the whispers grow louder, demanding justice and resolution. But as the shadow of the gang stretches over these cases, the veil of mystery remains firmly in place, making the quest for truth an ongoing battle against silence, speculation, and time itself. The echoes of these unsolved crimes continue to resonate through the city streets, their narratives incomplete, their conclusions yet unwritten.

Unsolved crimes linked to notorious gangs such as the Burger Bar Boys present a daunting challenge to law enforcement agencies. The complex web of secrecy, loyalty, and fear within gang cultures forms an intimidating barrier for investigators. This part delves into the labyrinthine path of challenges that law enforcement faces when working to untangle these cold cases, revealing the intricate dynamics of gang-related investigations.

A significant hurdle in these investigations is the ubiquitous 'code of silence' within gang culture. Gang members often refuse to cooperate with law enforcement, even when they become victims of violence themselves. This practice stems from a deep-seated distrust of the police and a commitment to self-preservation within the gang. It creates an ominous wall of silence that protects the perpetrators and leaves investigators with little more than circumstantial evidence and second-hand accounts to guide their inquiries.

Take, for example, the case of the double shooting in Aston. Despite the shooting occurring in a populated area, few witnesses came forward. The code of silence was so pervasive that even victims were hesitant to assist law enforcement. This lack of cooperation greatly hampered the investigation, allowing the perpetrators to slip through the fingers of justice.

In addition to the code of silence, another significant challenge is witness intimidation. Many of those who might have critical information fear retaliation from gang members if they cooperate with the police. The pervasive climate of fear often silences potential witnesses, leaving investigators to piece together the jigsaw puzzle of a crime with numerous missing pieces.

The unsolved murder of Daniel Turner is a chilling example of this. Despite the incident happening outside a crowded nightclub, the investigation was stymied by a lack of reliable eyewitnesses. The fear of reprisal from the Burger Bar Boys was a palpable barrier that hindered the pursuit of justice, rendering the case cold.

Moreover, a lack of tangible evidence poses another hurdle in solving these crimes. Gang-related crimes are often committed with meticulous planning, leaving little trace behind. In the case of the kidnapped businessman, for instance, the absence of any conclusive evidence linked to the Burger Bar Boys stalled the case indefinitely.

To tackle these challenges, law enforcement agencies use a combination of tried-and-tested and innovative strategies. For instance, they work closely with community organisations to build trust and encourage community members to come forward with information. New technologies, such as advancements in forensic science and data analysis, are also increasingly being employed to decipher crime patterns, analyse evidence, and create connections that may have previously been overlooked.

Law enforcement agencies also collaborate with national and international counterparts to exchange intelligence and share best practices. In the case of the Burger Bar Boys, this collaboration often extends to the sharing of information about the gang's operations outside Birmingham.

Despite these robust strategies and resources, solving gang-related cold cases remains an arduous task. The shadows cast by the Burger Bar Boys across these unsolved cases serve as a stark reminder of the investigative challenges that lie within the intricate and often closed world of gang culture. However, as technology and investigative techniques evolve, and as the resolve of law enforcement agencies strengthens, the hope for justice continues to flicker, illuminating the long and winding path towards truth.

Cold cases linked to the Burger Bar Boys represent an open wound in the heart of Birmingham, a stark reminder of lives disrupted and justice yet unserved. These cases, etched in the annals of the city's history, form a solemn narrative of resilience and unyielding pursuit of truth, a tale of a community's collective quest for justice.

At the forefront of this quest are the victims' families. Left in the wake of unsolved crimes, they grapple with a lingering sorrow that only the resolution of these cases can mollify. They confront not just the pain of losing a loved one but also the torment of not knowing who was responsible or why it happened. Their pursuit for answers persists, driven by a desire for closure and a hope that justice will prevent others from experiencing the same suffering.

The case of the teenager, gunned down on a quiet Birmingham street, serves as a poignant example. His family has spent years seeking answers, tirelessly advocating for the investigation to continue, their calls for justice echoing through the corridors of power. Their unwavering commitment serves as a powerful testament to the human desire for justice and closure.

Yet, the impact of these unsolved cases reverberates beyond the victims' families, influencing the wider Birmingham community. Each unresolved case fuels a climate of fear and mistrust, casting a shadow over the community's sense of security and peace. Addressing these unsolved cases is essential for restoring a sense of safety and communal harmony.

Law enforcement agencies recognise this importance. Despite the passing years, the cases are not forgotten, filed away and left to gather dust. Instead, they remain active, each case a quest, a commitment from the police to the community they serve. Unsolved does not mean unattended; rather, it represents a challenge to meet, a resolution to find.

New leads are pursued, old evidence re-examined through the lens of advanced forensic techniques, and renewed efforts made to seek out witnesses who might have been too afraid to come forward at the time. Special cold case units continue to pore over these cases, fuelled by a combination of dogged determination, an understanding of the impact of these unresolved cases on the community, and the belief that justice, no matter how delayed, serves a vital role in societal healing.

The cold case of the missing woman serves as an example. The case, initially thought to be a mere disappearance, was revisited years later when new information surfaced, suggesting the involvement of the Burger Bar Boys. Despite the passage of time, the investigators embraced the opportunity to possibly solve the case, renewing the hope of justice for the woman's distraught family and a city that still remembers.

The unsolved mysteries tied to the Burger Bar Boys represent more than a chapter in Birmingham's criminal history. They are a testament to the complex challenges of investigating gang crimes, the resilient spirit of those who seek justice, and the importance of resolving these cases for the sake of the victims, their families, and the community. While the shadows of the Burger Bar Boys still linger over these cases, the quest for justice continues, its flame fueled by the hope that each resolved case brings. As long as these cases remain, so too does the commitment to seeking truth, to bringing resolution, and ultimately, to ensuring that the echoes of the past continue to drive the quest for justice in the present and future.

THE POWER VACUUM: THE DECLINE OF THE BURGER BAR BOYS

Over the years, the Burger Bar Boys had dominated Birmingham's underworld with their illicit operations, leaving an indelible mark on the city's history. Yet, like the rise and fall of empires, the once-fearsome gang began to crumble, and their reign of terror started to falter. The causes of the gang's decline were complex and multifaceted, and this exploration begins with a look at the internal issues that contributed to their downfall.

The first and perhaps most critical issue was leadership crises. The gang's structure was primarily hierarchical, with a small group of influential figures at the top. When alleged key members such as Marcus Ellis and Nathan Antonio Martin, who were implicated in high-profile crimes, including the tragic New Year shootings of Charlene Ellis and Letisha Shakespeare, were convicted and imprisoned, it created a power vacuum at the top. The absence of these figures led to confusion, infighting, and lack of direction, contributing significantly to the gang's decline.

Factionalism was another potent factor that played into their weakening hold. As the Burger Bar Boys grew, so did the rivalries and disagreements within the gang. What was once a united front began to fracture into smaller sub-groups, each vying for power and control. The result was a fragmented organisation, lacking the unity and cohesiveness that had once made it a formidable force in Birmingham's underworld.

Further exacerbating the internal issues was disorganisation, a common problem faced by many criminal gangs over time. As law enforcement cracked down, communication between gang members became more challenging. Coupled with a lack of strong leadership, this led to chaos and disarray. Organised crime requires a certain level of coordination and discipline, and when this started to falter within the Burger Bar Boys, it marked the beginning of the end.

External pressures were also significant in the decline of the Burger Bar Boys. Law enforcement had been gradually intensifying their efforts against the gang. Operations like Ventara, among others, were successful in arresting and convicting numerous gang members, disrupting their operations, and creating a climate of fear and uncertainty within the gang. The heightened pressure from law enforcement also deterred potential new members from joining, further weakening the gang's strength and influence.

Societal changes also contributed to the weakening of the gang. Public sentiment against the gang was high, especially following high-profile crimes such as the New Year shootings. Community organisations and local leaders were vocal in their opposition to the gang, leading initiatives aimed at deterring youth from joining and advocating for increased law enforcement action against the gang.

Lastly, rival gangs saw the Burger Bar Boys' waning power as an opportunity to assert their own dominance. Gangs like the Johnson Crew seized the opportunity to expand their territories and take over some of the Burger Bar Boys' operations, further accelerating their decline.

The downfall of the Burger Bar Boys was not an overnight occurrence but a gradual erosion of power. The gang that had once held Birmingham in a vice-like grip was beginning to lose its hold, setting the stage for a power vacuum that would have significant implications for the city's underworld.

The decline of the Burger Bar Boys led to a significant reshaping of Birmingham's underworld. As the gang's grip weakened, a power vacuum emerged, bringing with it a new wave of uncertainty and chaos. This section explores the immediate aftermath of this decline and how the void was handled within the criminal landscape of Birmingham.

One of the most immediate and visible impacts was the rise in gang violence. With the Burger Bar Boys no longer able to maintain their territories, rival gangs saw an opportunity to seize control. Gangs such as the Johnson Crew and others moved in quickly, hoping to establish dominance. The result was a violent struggle for control that led to a spike in gang-related crimes across the city. These included turf wars, drive-by shootings, and retaliatory attacks, all contributing to a volatile and unpredictable situation.

This struggle was not just confined to established gangs. The power vacuum also saw the emergence of new gangs, each hoping to carve out a piece of the underworld for themselves. These smaller, often more volatile groups added another layer of complexity to the already chaotic scene. Many were formed by former Burger Bar Boys members who had splintered off during the gang's decline, bringing with them a deep-seated resentment and a desire for power.

The impact of the power vacuum was felt acutely by the communities that the Burger Bar Boys had once controlled. Residents, many of whom had already suffered years under the gang's rule, found themselves caught in the crossfire of this new wave of gang violence. Innocent bystanders became victims, and the fear that once permeated these communities during the height of the Burger Bar Boys' reign returned in full force.

In response to these developments, law enforcement agencies were forced to adapt and revise their strategies. With the Burger Bar Boys' decline and the rise of new gangs, the criminal landscape had changed, and the tactics that had worked against a single, dominant gang were less effective in this new environment.

The West Midlands Police, in particular, had to contend with the increased violence and the surge of new gangs. They launched operations aimed at curbing the rising violence, including increased patrols, intelligence gathering, and cooperation with community leaders. They also initiated programmes aimed at deterring young people from joining these emerging gangs, focusing on education and providing alternative pathways.

Nevertheless, the law enforcement agencies faced significant challenges. The surge in violence stretched their resources thin, and the fluid, unpredictable nature of the new gangs made them difficult to pin down. Yet, despite these challenges, they remained committed to restoring peace and order to the city.

The immediate aftermath of the Burger Bar Boys' decline revealed the complex dynamics of gang power and control. The void that the gang left behind was not just a territorial one, but also a social and political vacuum, impacting every facet of Birmingham's underworld. As the city grappled with this new reality, the stage was set for a prolonged period of instability and change.

As the dust settled from the initial upheaval that followed the decline of the Burger Bar Boys, the long-term implications for Birmingham's communities began to emerge. The landscape of the city's underworld had changed dramatically, and with it, so too did the lives of those who had been under the gang's shadow.

Crime rates, particularly violent and gang-related crime, fluctuated significantly in the years following the Burger Bar Boys' decline. The initial spike, driven by territorial disputes and the emergence of new gangs, eventually began to stabilise as law enforcement agencies adapted to the new status quo. However, this stability came at a high cost. Increased policing and more aggressive crime-fighting strategies brought their own set of challenges, from community relations to the potential for civil liberties violations.

The community dynamics also underwent a transformation. The fear and tension that had once pervaded neighbourhoods controlled by the Burger Bar Boys began to ease, replaced by a cautious optimism. Community leaders, freed from the spectre of gang intimidation, were able to take a more proactive role in shaping their neighbourhoods.

Public perception of gang activity, influenced by the Burger Bar Boys' reign and subsequent fall, also evolved. People became more vigilant, and there was an increased awareness of the dangers and consequences of gang involvement. This heightened awareness led

116

to a strengthened community resolve to prevent the rise of another gang that could fill the vacuum left by the Burger Bar Boys.

In response to these changing dynamics, a variety of preventive measures and initiatives were introduced, both by the community and by law enforcement agencies. These initiatives aimed at mitigating the risk of a new gang rising from the ashes of the Burger Bar Boys and perpetuating the cycle of violence.

Community-based programs saw a particular increase, with efforts focusing on providing alternatives to gang involvement for the youth. These included educational opportunities, vocational training, mentorship programs, and recreational activities. The aim was to offer positive, constructive pathways for young people who might otherwise be lured into the gang lifestyle.

Law enforcement agencies, for their part, focused on improving their strategies. They worked on building stronger relationships with communities, recognizing that a cooperative, trust-based approach was more effective than an adversarial one. Efforts were also made to enhance intelligence-gathering capabilities to preempt and disrupt any potential gang activity.

Over time, these initiatives began to yield results. The rate of gang-related crime saw a gradual decline, and the sense of community strengthened in previously gang-dominated areas. However, the spectre of the Burger Bar Boys, and the void their decline left, remained a constant reminder of the need for vigilance and proactive community engagement.

The decline of the Burger Bar Boys marked a pivotal chapter in Birmingham's history. It was a period of turbulence and transition, of violence and power struggles, but it also became a catalyst for change and a platform for community resilience. As the city continues to navigate the aftermath, the legacy of the Burger Bar Boys serves as a stark reminder of the destructive impact of gang culture and the unyielding resolve of a community determined to reclaim its streets.

The story of the Burger Bar Boys' rise and fall is more than just a narrative of a gang's dominance and decline. It's a testament to the enduring spirit of Birmingham's communities and their relentless pursuit of safety and stability. As the city moves forward, its future, no longer shadowed by the Burger Bar Boys, is testament to the resilience of its people and their undying hope for a peaceful, prosperous   Birmingham.

LEGACY OF VIOLENCE: THE LASTING IMPACT OF THE BURGER BAR BOYS

While the Burger Bar Boys may no longer command the same power they once did, their imprint on Birmingham's underworld is far from erased. Their legacy, shaped by violence, territorial control, and illicit activities, continues to cast a long, unsettling shadow over the city.

The legacy of the Burger Bar Boys doesn't merely rest on their past actions, but more ominously on the fear they instilled. The trauma inflicted by the gang is still fresh in the minds of many, and the narrative of fear continues to be perpetuated. Nighttime stories of the gang's ruthless tactics have been passed down from older generations to younger ones, fueling a continuous cycle of apprehension.

This fear has seeped into the fabric of everyday life. For instance, in certain areas of the city once dominated by the gang, residents remain guarded, always watching over their shoulders, a behaviour ingrained from the days when a wrong move could attract the gang's wrath. This chronic vigilance has disrupted the sense of community, with trust among neighbours eroded, replaced by an invisible wall of anxiety.

Moreover, the gang's influence is perceptible in the enduring territorial divisions within Birmingham. The invisible boundaries they established – which streets belonged to whom and which areas were no-go zones for rival gangs – linger in the collective city memory. While the direct enforcement of these territorial lines has diminished, residents still recognize and respect them. For some, crossing these invisible lines feels like a violation, a holdover from the times when such a step could mean entering a lethal conflict.

The Burger Bar Boys also impacted the city's underworld, establishing a violent, win-at-all-costs blueprint for criminal behaviour. Their use of firearms, willingness to engage in violent conflicts, and ostentatious displays of wealth set a precedent that future gangs would emulate. The Burger Bar Boys, thus, didn't just dominate the city during their peak – they changed the rules of the game entirely.

This model they set up reverberates through Birmingham's criminal underworld, shaping the way gangs operate even today. Newer gangs seeking to establish their authority often find themselves adopting tactics that the Burger Bar Boys pioneered. This emulation, whether conscious or not, demonstrates the lasting influence of the Burger Bar Boys on the city's gang culture.

In the larger cultural context, the Burger Bar Boys have also etched a lasting mark. Their notoriety has been picked up by media and popular culture, often romanticising the gang lifestyle and its codes. The reality of the brutality and the socio-economic impacts on the community, however, get lost in the shuffle, leaving behind a skewed representation that further cements the gang's influence.

Indeed, the echoes of the Burger Bar Boys' reign continue to resonate through Birmingham's streets, a testament to the gang's lingering influence. Despite their decline, they have left a cultural and psychological imprint that will take much time and effort to erase.

The Burger Bar Boys, during their reign, significantly disrupted the socioeconomic fabric of Birmingham. The profound impact they had, and continue to have, extends beyond the realm of crime, trickling into various other aspects of life, including employment, education, public health, and housing.

Job prospects in areas dominated by the gang suffered tremendously during their reign. Businesses often found themselves in the crossfire of the gang's violent turf wars, discouraging entrepreneurs from setting up shop and established businesses from continuing operations. The frequent conflicts and associated risks deterred investment and led to job losses, contributing to economic stagnation in the gang's territories. Even now, years after the Burger Bar Boys' decline, the economic landscape of these areas remains blighted by the gang's past activities.

Education suffered a similar fate. The presence of the gang made attending school a risky proposition for many youngsters. Absenteeism and drop-out rates escalated, largely driven by safety concerns. Moreover, the lure of quick, albeit illicit, wealth presented by the gang life diverted many young minds from the path of education. The long-term impacts of these disruptions are evident in the lower educational attainment levels and the diminished human capital in areas once under the gang's control.

These educational outcomes feed into a vicious cycle. With reduced access to quality education, residents of these areas are less likely to secure well-paying jobs, which in turn increases the likelihood of crime, contributing to the continuation of the gang's legacy. Breaking this cycle requires sustained investment in education and youth services, something the city has struggled with.

In terms of public health, the Burger Bar Boys' activities have left a significant impact. The violence associated with the gang has led to both physical injuries and mental trauma, putting a strain on healthcare services. Furthermore, the gang's involvement in drug trafficking has contributed to substance misuse problems within the community, leading to a myriad of health issues, including addiction and drug-related diseases. These health concerns persist long after the gang's decline, with drug addiction proving particularly hard to tackle.

The influence of the gang has been felt in housing too. Areas known to be the gang's stronghold have often been stigmatised, leading to lower property values. For residents, this has resulted in reduced wealth and difficulty in securing loans using their property as collateral. For the community as a whole, the stigma has led to reduced investment in housing and public infrastructure, further entrenching these areas in a cycle of deprivation.

The long shadow of the Burger Bar Boys also extends to social relationships and community cohesion. The fear and mistrust sown by the gang have had a lasting effect on how communities interact, often leading to social isolation and fragmentation.

Overall, the socioeconomic impacts of the Burger Bar Boys' reign have been far-reaching, perpetuating a cycle of deprivation that continues to be felt by the Birmingham community. Overcoming these deep-rooted issues is a monumental task, requiring not only significant resources but also a fundamental change in how these communities are supported and invested in.

Despite the far-reaching impacts of the Burger Bar Boys, there have been considerable efforts to mend the broken societal fabric and rejuvenate the communities affected by the gang's activities. These endeavours, coming from various quarters, including the government, non-profit organisations, and the community members themselves, aim at both healing the wounds and preventing the re-emergence of such destructive forces.

The government has played a critical role in this recovery process. Policing efforts, which were initially focused on suppressing gang activity, have evolved to incorporate a more community-centric approach. The authorities have recognized the importance of winning the trust of the community to effectively combat crime and foster social cohesion. Initiatives like neighbourhood policing, which involves officers working closely with local residents to identify and address issues, have been adopted to promote a sense of security and community ownership.

Investments in education and youth services have also been significant in the government's rehabilitation strategy. Schools in affected areas have been provided with additional resources to tackle absenteeism and improve educational outcomes. Youth services, which suffered from chronic underfunding during the reign of the Burger Bar Boys, have received renewed attention. By offering constructive activities and mentorship, these programs aim to divert the youth from the allure of gang life and towards more promising futures.

In addition to the government's efforts, numerous non-profit organisations have been instrumental in the healing process. These entities have tackled various issues, from providing support to victims of gang violence to offering drug rehabilitation services and job training programs. They have also been crucial in bridging the trust gap between the communities and the authorities, serving as intermediaries and advocates for the residents.

The community itself has been an integral part of the recovery process. There has been a resurgence of community organisations, driven by individuals determined to reclaim their neighbourhoods from the shadow of the Burger Bar Boys. These organisations, often run by local residents, have been involved in everything from neighbourhood watch initiatives to community development projects. By fostering a sense of unity and collective responsibility, these groups are working to rebuild the social bonds that were eroded during the gang's reign.

These efforts, however, are just the start of a long journey. Healing the wounds inflicted by the Burger Bar Boys and reversing the socioeconomic impact of their activities is a daunting task that will take years, if not decades. Yet, the concerted efforts from various stakeholders have shown that progress is possible.

The story of the Burger Bar Boys serves as a stark reminder of how a criminal entity can disrupt society. Yet, it also highlights the resilience of communities and their ability to come together to repair and rebuild. The legacy of the gang will linger, but so will the stories of recovery and resurgence.

Ultimately, the tale of Birmingham's rise from the ashes left by the Burger Bar Boys isn't just about overcoming the impacts of a criminal enterprise. It's a testament to human resilience, the power of community, and the unyielding pursuit of a safer, more prosperous future. As we delve deeper into this story, we can draw lessons and inspirations that extend beyond Birmingham, resonating with any community around the world that has faced, or continues to face, similar   challenges.

AFTERWORD

As we reach the end of this dark and tumultuous journey through the streets of Birmingham, tracing the rise and fall of the notorious Burger Bar Boys, it is worth pausing to reflect on the lessons gleaned from this complex tale. The twenty chapters of "Gangland Birmingham: The Rise and Fall of the Burger Bar Boys" do more than merely recount the chronicles of a gang; they tell a cautionary tale of the interplay between systemic neglect, violence, desperation, and ambition.

The narrative of the Burger Bar Boys is a stark window into the birth and evolution of a gang, shaped by the socio-economic pressures that bear down on the most deprived corners of our urban environments. Each chapter, in its way, underscores the profound consequences of allowing these pressures to go unchecked. The allure of power, camarity, and material gain, starkly juxtaposed with the brutal devaluation of life, paints an unsettling picture of an alternate society existing within our own, one ruled by its own grim codes and laws.

From their inception in the neglected urban sprawl of Birmingham to their blood-stained peak and their inevitable downfall, the Burger Bar Boys stand as a testament to the all-consuming nature of gang life. A subculture where brutality, fear, and a chilling disregard for life is the norm, and where compassion is often viewed as weakness.

Chapter by harrowing chapter, we have explored the criminal activities that earned the Burger Bar Boys their reputation and gripped Birmingham in a state of near-constant fear. The terrifying reality of gunplay, the vast and destructive drug trafficking operations, and the notorious Aston Shootings have all underscored the profound societal costs that such a gang inflicts upon a community. But perhaps even more importantly, they have highlighted the resilience and fortitude of the community of

Birmingham, standing firm in the face of a rising tide of violence and fear.

The influences of the Burger Bar Boys extended far beyond the physical realm, infiltrating the cultural fabric of the society they operated within. Their mark on music, film, and popular culture demonstrated the potency of their legacy, a dark fascination that often masked the grim reality of their deeds. Even though the Burger Bar Boys are no longer a functioning entity, their shadow continues to loom over Birmingham's cultural and societal narratives.

Amidst the tales of violence and crime, however, there are rays of hope that pierce through the darkness. The stories of those few who managed to escape the gang's grip, who chose to seek redemption, show us that the cycle of violence is not inevitable. It is a testament to the human spirit's capacity for change, a beacon of hope in an otherwise bleak landscape.

In the aftermath of the gang's decline, we've examined the power vacuum that emerged, the reshaping of Birmingham's underworld, and the repercussions for the community. The decline of a gang does not instantly erase its footprint; it leaves behind a complex web of socio-economic impacts that continue to shape the affected areas. Yet, even in the face of such adversity, we see the relentless efforts of Birmingham's community to heal and rebuild. Through government initiatives, non-profit organisations, and the sheer willpower of its citizens, Birmingham continues to fight the lingering spectre of the Burger Bar Boys.

Reflecting on the overarching narrative of the Burger Bar Boys, it becomes clear that this story is a dire warning from history. It underscores the perilous consequences of societal neglect and the dangerous path that desperate and marginalised youths can be forced down. The tale of the Burger Bar Boys is a stark reminder that lack of opportunities, education, and proactive interventions can lead to the birth of such dangerous entities.

However, the story is also a testament to resilience, redemption, and the enduring hope for change. It highlights the potential for transformation, not just on an individual level but on a community-wide scale. It points to the need for systemic change, the importance of providing opportunities for youth, and the immense value in supporting environments that nurture rather than neglect.

In conclusion, "Gangland Birmingham: The Rise and Fall of the Burger Bar Boys" presents a dark tapestry woven from stories of violence, power, fear, and resilience. It serves as both a stark reminder of our past failings and a potent catalyst for future change. As we reflect upon the saga of the Burger Bar Boys, let us remember the steep price of systemic neglect and the profound impacts of gang culture. However, let us also remember the stories of redemption, the ongoing efforts to heal a wounded community, and the continued fight for a safer, more equitable future.

The tale of the Burger Bar Boys stands as a cautionary testament to the dangerous allure of gang life and the enduring impacts of its violence. However, it is also a story of hope, of communities rallying together in the face of adversity, and of the potential for change. Let this book serve not just as a historical account, but also as a call to action, an appeal for understanding, and a beacon of hope. A reminder that while our past may be marred by darkness, our future is yet unwritten, and within our power to change.

ABOUT THE AUTHOR

L. Brickley

Lee Brickley is a prolific investigator and author with more than 20 books currently in publication. To read more from this author, simply search "Lee Brickley" on Amazon.

Printed in Great Britain
by Amazon